Earthing Christologies

FAITH AND SCHOLARSHIP
COLLOQUIES SERIES

Earthing Christologies

From Jesus' Parables to
Jesus the Parable

Edited by
James H. Charlesworth
and Walter P. Weaver

Faith and Scholarship Colloquies

Trinity Press International   Valley Forge, Pa.

First Published 1995

Trinity Press International
P.O. Box 851
Valley Forge, PA 19482-0851

Cover Design by Jim Gerhard

Library of Congress Cataloging-in-Publication Data

Earthing christologies : from Jesus' parables to Jesus the parable /
edited by James H. Charlesworth and Walter P. Weaver.
    p.   cm. – (Faith and scholarship colloquies)
    Rev. ed of: Perspectives on Christology. c1989.
    Includes bibliographical references and index.
    ISBN 1-56338-119-2 (pbk.)
    1. Jesus Christ–Person and offices.   I. Charlesworth, James H.
II. Weaver, Walter P.   III. Perspectives on Christology.
IV. Series.
BT202.P44   1995
232'.8–dc20
                                                                95-30167
                                                                CIP

Printed in the United States of America

95   96   97   98   99   10   9   8   7   6   5   4   3   2   1

To our parents
Jean and Arthur Charlesworth
and
Elizabeth and Stacy Weaver
who gave us life
and
models for living it

Contents

Contributors

HUGH ANDERSON is Emeritus Professor New Testament Language, Literature, and Theology at the University of Edinburgh. He held the Pendergrass Chair in Religion at Florida Southern College in the academic year 1987–1988.

JAMES H. CHARLESWORTH is George L. Collord Professor of New Testament Language and Literature at Princeton Theological Seminary and Director of the PTS Dead Sea Scrolls Project.

LEANDER E. KECK is the former Dean of the Divinity School, Yale University, and Winkley Professor of Biblical Theology.

WALTER P. WEAVER is Chairman of the Humanities Division, the Department of Religion and Philosophy, and Pendergrass Professor of Religion at Florida Southern College.

Series Description

Faith and Scholarship Colloquies

This series explores the boundaries where faith and academic study intersect. At these borders, the sharp edge of current biblical scholarship is allowed to cut theologically and pose its often challenging questions for traditional faith. The series includes contributions from leading scholars in contemporary biblical studies. As Christian faith seeks to send a word on target in our day, as powerful as those in the past, it needs to sharpen its perception and proclamation from honest and truthful insights in human knowledge, from first-century archaeology to modern linguistics.

Acknowledgments

There are any number of persons who have helped make possible this collection of papers. First, of course, are the participants in the original symposium, who have generously provided updated versions of their work. The president of Florida Southern College at the time (1988), Dr. Robert A. Davis, has provided unstinting support to make possible the symposia series in the first instance. Without that support it would not be possible to carry on these significant dialogues. The excellent services of the secretary of the Department of Religion and Philosophy, Mrs. Beverly Johnson, were also of unsurpassed value in preparation of the original volume for Exodus Press. And, finally, I express thanks to my colleagues in the Department of Religion and Philosophy who continue to give their time and energy to the successful management of the symposia and often to active participation in the form of papers.

I also wish to acknowledge the generosity and many kindnesses of the Center of Theological Inquiry at Princeton for its gracious hosting of my sabbatical leave in the spring semester of 1994. While the main project lay elsewhere, there was sufficient opportunity for James Charlesworth and me to complete the reediting of this volume for publication in the Faith and Scholarship Colloquies series.

Walter P. Weaver

Foreword

These essays were first published in 1989 by Exodus Press in Nashville, Tennessee. They have now been revised and updated for publication by Trinity Press International. Professor Weaver and I are appreciative to Exodus Press for the permission to republish these chapters in a revised form. I am delighted to see them circulated to a wider audience. Each is well written, and the choice of words and perspective shared by Anderson, Weaver, and Keck is outstanding; at times — as I prepared the chapters for revising — I was moved by the carefully couched expressions (prose often broke into poetry and symbolic language).

Each of us — the head of the Humanities Division at Florida Southern College, the former Dean of Yale Divinity School, and the former head of the New Testament department at Edinburgh University — are convinced that Bultmann, the most influential New Testament scholar of this century, was unduly and unperceptively critical of the historical and ethnic dimensions of the New Testament. All of us reject his historical negativism and his controverted assertion that the Jesus of history was only a presupposition of New Testament theology. Yet with him we acknowledge that faith must not be, and never has been, dependent on the facts of history (*bruta facta*) or on the historian's genius for reconstructing the past. The mystery of the hidden presence of God in the teaching and life of Jesus cannot be obtained through historical research. This mystery and continuing power for renewal in our lives and our world cannot be derived from even the most perspicacious clarification of Jesus' obvious teachings and activities, like the proclamation of God's rule (the kingdom of God), his understanding of love and exhortation to love our "neighbors" (including our enemies) as ourselves, his penchant for calling God Abba ("Father"), his healings, his forgiveness, his siding always with the poor and outcast against the overbearing establishment, and his ultimate loyalty to God even to death on a cross. The mystery resides in his oneness with God and his power to call us to share in that oneness.

As Professor Weaver and I send this book out to be read by all who are interested, we do not wish to conceal a dream we have for the church and the world. May the church and the world be more open to the stimulating and freeing insights obtained, through study and meditation, by the scholars — all of whom are Christians — who have labored on the perennial question of why that Jew of the ancient Near Eastern world so powerfully influences us of the modern Western world.

Volumes in the Faith and Scholarship Colloquies series attempt to wed the insights of scholarship with the inquisitiveness of faith (*fides quaerens intellectum*). The title of the present volume is reminiscent of a speech in 1910 by Wilhelm Bousset. In it he judiciously perceived that "Jesus did not only create the symbols of the Gospel in essentials, but became symbol Himself."[1] As Anderson, Keck, Weaver, and I invite our readers to explore the continuity of the historical Jesus and confessed Christ, let us contemplate what it means for our own lives to perceive in the parables of our earth the Parable from above.

James H. Charlesworth

NOTE

1. W. Bousset, "The Significance of the Personality of Jesus for Belief," *Report of the Fifth International Congress for Free Christianity and Religious Progress: Berlin 1910* (Berlin-Schöneberg: Protestantischer Schriftenvertrieb, 1911), 15.

Introduction

Hugh Anderson

In the course of the discussion periods that followed the presentation of each of these essays, it became clear there was broad agreement among contributors on certain key issues, such as the continuing legitimacy of Jesus Research and the decisive significance of the resurrection for the church's proclamation. There emerged also, however, considerable divergence of opinion on several basic concerns. Given that the primary intention of the Gospel writers is not to offer a biography of Jesus (certainly not in any modern sense of the word "biography"), how much can we recover from the Gospels of the actual life of Jesus of Nazareth? How does such knowledge of Jesus as can be gleaned from the New Testament relate to believers' faith in the crucified and risen Christ? Have we the means of gauging Jesus' own understanding of his person and mission? What are we to make of the ancient, traditional notion of Christ as the God-man, of the union in him of two natures, divine and human?

This last question stood at the very center of the creedal controversies in which the church so passionately engaged in the third and fourth centuries. The struggle to ward off heretical tendencies and to encapsulate and define orthodox Christian doctrine in a short but comprehensive confessional statement culminated in the Chalcedonian Formula and the earlier Nicene

Creed, more familiar to most people through the churches' liturgies today: "We believe in One God, the Father Almighty and in One Lord Jesus Christ, the only begotten Son of God, begotten of his Father before all worlds, God of God, Light of Light, Very God of Very God, begotten, not made, being of one substance with the Father, by whom all things were made."

The two-nature conception of the person (and work) of Christ expressed here arose directly and inevitably from the cultural context in which the great leaders of the church lived and thought and believed. The terms and categories in which the ancient debate about Christology was couched were part and parcel of the metaphysical system espoused by Aristotle; a great deal hinged on the interpretation of such rather complex and ambiguous Greek words as *ousia* ("substance") and *hypostasis* (a precise English equivalent is not easy to come by! Perhaps "a real or actual being contrasted to what merely seems to be") or the Latin *persona* ("someone who plays a part in human affairs").

The Greek terms *ousia* and *hypostasis* are very rare in the New Testament. Where they do occur, they are not "philosophically loaded," so to speak (e.g., in Luke 15:12 *ousia* means "substance" in the sense of "wealth" or "property"; in 2 Cor. 11:17 and Heb. 3:14 *hypostasis* means "assurance" or "confidence"). The exception is Hebrews 1:3, where the Son (Christ) is described as "the exact imprint of God's *very being*" (*hypostasis*). Hebrews 1:3 is in fact an early milestone on the way to the great creedal controversies of later centuries, in which words like *ousia* and *hypostasis* figured prominently. In wrestling with the mystery of the person of Christ, leaders of the church had then to fit him as best they could into their own thought-world of Aristotelian philosophy. And so must we, some sixteen centuries later, denizens as we are of an unimaginably different thought-world. So true is it that each generation has to wrestle afresh with new adaptations of the inherited traditions relating to Christ's person and work, new concepts, symbols, and images or models, in accordance with its own particular understanding of God, humanity, and the universe.

I have no wish to imply by what has just been said that we have nothing whatever to learn any more from the church's ancient creedal controversies and confessions. We should not lightly dismiss the efforts of a number of modern theologians with expertise in patristics (e.g., T. F. Torrance, E. L. Mascall, J. Moltmann), to expound and explain the various arguments of the church fathers concerning the divine-human nature in Christ, especially as these bear on the doctrine of the Trinity. The works of the fathers do at least reflect vividly for us the church's heroic, albeit often bitter, fight to save "the faith once for all delivered to the saints" from floundering in the quicksands of many a weird, heretical distortion of the gospel of Jesus Christ proclaimed in Scripture. As we noted, in waging the struggle to formulate orthodox Christian doctrine, they were bound within the parameters of the philosophic "temper" of their own time and were led to create the two-nature Christology out of the metaphysics of Aristotle.

Now readers will search in vain in the following pages for any treatment of the two-nature christological model. The essayists do not, of course, discount a continuing validity for such treatment. But their principal focus lies elsewhere, aware as they are that many in the churches at the present time, and not only professional theologians, find the philosophical language of the third and fourth centuries archaic, unfamiliar, and unacceptable. If today the christological debate is in as much, if not more, ferment than ever, it is not through wrangling about how we should perceive the meaning of philosophically abstract terms like *ousia* ("substance"), *hypostasis, persona* ("person"), "nature" or "natures." Rather the search is on for quite other categories or models for understanding the person and work of Jesus Christ. It is a search that stems from the great cultural revolution, of which we are the heirs. Its roots can be traced as far back as the Renaissance to such pioneers of the free spirit of intellectual enquiry as Erasmus. But it has burgeoned prolifically since the rise of Rationalism in the Enlightenment of the latter part of the eighteenth century.

The discovery in that period of the importance and power of the human faculty of critical reasoning produced widespread movements of revolt against all forms of dogmatism, authoritarianism, and imperialism in church and state. In the wake of the Enlightenment came momentous social and political events that helped largely to shape the course of the history of the West: the French Revolution with its slogan, *liberté, égalité, fraternité;* and the breakaway of the young American colonies from the increasingly despised British monarch, George III, "the sceptred tyrant" (Thomas Jefferson in a letter to John Randolph, November 1775), and the eventual foundation of a new nation.

Closer to our interest here, however, is the profound effect the Enlightenment had in the intellectual sphere, particularly in the arena of theology and Christology. Pre-critical views of the Bible as a sacrosanct repository of fixed and immutable dogmas, or the vehicle of the untouchable "facts of salvation," were exposed to the cold blast of uninhibited critical investigation of the scriptural texts. Preoccupation with doctrine or closed doctrinal systems gave way to intense exploration of the *history* of early Christianity. Accurate reconstruction of the past life of Jesus and of the early church, by the use of all critical tools available and indeed all those at the disposal of the secular historian, became the order of the day in many quarters. Not in *all* quarters, we must add, since to this very day the forces of conservatism have resolutely resisted the historical-critical approach to Scripture, and perhaps never more stubbornly than now. Conservatives have consistently held that by its unique nature as in all its parts God's infallible Word, the Bible, should be placed in a reserved area and "No Entry" signs erected against prying and probing historical critics.

It goes without saying that the vigor of James Charlesworth's historical-critical method as applied to what he calls "Jesus Research" and the study of Christian origins is quite unlikely to appeal to fundamentalists or to people of strong conservative tendency: customarily recognizing no difference between matters of historical fact and faith in the Bible and accepting all biblical statements as *indivisibly* the truth (but what is truth?), they see no need to try to penetrate behind the texts to rediscover and build up a picture of what really happened. In my judgment, however, and I am sure in that of my colleagues, in pursuing historical Jesus Research with all stringency, Charlesworth is simply being faithful to the claim of Christianity to be a *historical* religion, historical in the unusual sense that from the beginning Christian faith and thought centered in Jesus, "born of a woman, born under the Law," born a Jew, that is.

In view of the foregoing observations, it is not surprising that the decisive issues that emerge in this book are as follows: how far can we go in recovering the historical life of the man Jesus (or, for that matter of the apostle Paul and the earliest Christian communities), considering the limited nature of our resources within the biblical canon? Have we extra-canonical sources of information to assist us? Since Jesus' ministry and message was through and through God-directed, must not the "Jesus researcher" who would do his subject justice be a theologian, open to the suprahistorical dimension, to the transcendent? What is the connection between the Jesus of history and the Christ of the church's faith and preaching? These issues and numerous cognate problems have been predominant in recent years. When one considers the welter of conflicting opinions on them, it is only to be expected that my colleagues and I should differ in our individual perceptions.

But (and this is crucial) we are unanimously agreed that divergence of opinion in the theological or christological arena is a mark of health and vitality. Diversity of viewpoint makes for animated dialogue, and dialogue (not retreat into repetitive monologue) is the way forward to deeper understanding. When we refuse dialogue, prescind from any questions, and hide behind the shelter of an infallible book, we risk the stagnation and petrifaction of the biblical traditions and the traditions handed down to us across nearly two millennia of church history. Better far to put ourselves at risk by asking ever fresh questions of the New Testament writings and attempting brave new answers. Thereby we open up the possibility of new understandings of the New Testament witness to Jesus Christ and new encounters with Christ himself. And in any case genuine faith and the element of risk are inalienable companions. For my part, I find myself in broad agreement with the complaint made by Dr. John Bowden that one of the most serious faults of the churches has been to neglect the people who *think* and to take the populist line of pleasing the silent majority by refusing to rock the boat. In his preface to Bowden's book (*Jesus: The Unanswered Questions* [London: SCM Press, 1988]), Dr. David Jenkins, until recently the bishop of Durham, England, scathingly indicts "the posturing emperors of religious certainty and moral absolutism" as emperors without clothes.

I am not sure whether my fellow participants in the symposium would consider the charges leveled by Jenkins and Bowden as a too stern radical backlash to the conservatism that is on the rise at the moment. What I do know is that both they and I are at one in holding that in a subject so many-sided as

Christology, definitive or final solutions will continue to elude us. None of us would pretend that in our forays into the field of Christology, in this book and elsewhere, we have easy answers to offer. Rather our aim has been, as we hope, to advance comprehension, perhaps inch by inch, by promoting the asking of questions.

Protests may and will be made that the bounden duty of the Christian scholar no less than of the preacher is to hold up Christ as the all-sufficient Answer. Or that few in the churches are inclined to explore deep theological or christological problems, and the overwhelming majority, if they were to articulate their feelings, would want to be left to a simple faith, which were better undisturbed. To such protests I would reply: (1) To reflect on the meaning of the person and work of Christ is not the sole preserve of academic theologians. It is the constant right and obligation of the Christian community at large, as the body of Christ, to think, with the heart certainly, but no less with the mind, on the one who is its Head. The theologian may function as guide and counselor to the community's reflection, but the whole community ought to be involved, toward its greater maturity in Christ. (2) In the course of my ministry I have met men and women who were described as having a "simple faith." In coming to know them more intimately, I have invariably found that their faith was assuredly no facile or sunshine affair. Rather had it dawned for them at the end of "A Long Day's Journey into Night." And at an inestimable cost, through sorrow and suffering and loss, and many a dark hour of doubt and questioning! In Gethsemane, Jesus himself experienced doubt and prayed that the cup of suffering might pass from him, before he surrendered to the Father's will. The historic "secret," or one "secret," of how the gospel of Jesus Christ has made such a vast impact across the ages is that it confronts us with one who "knows our infirmities," who visits and embraces human existence most closely at the point of its awful ambiguity and vulnerability, its strange changes and chances, its sudden "sunset touches" and tragedies. One whose own uniquely good life was climaxed by a premature, painful, and violent death at the hands of malevolent and evil men! No answer is possible save to a question or questions previously asked. The cross of Christ has an unfathomable power (power in weakness) to elicit ultimate questions of why life in its iron(ic) reality is just as it is, of why we are here, and what is our destiny under God (is God a just God or not?). On these questions faith and reason (and I would add imagination) can work together for good to the deepening and enriching of our humanity and the enhancing of our character. Would not that be an answer, God-given and Christ-inspired, to our searching?

I have suggested that reflection on Christ's person and work is a function of the whole church. It is regrettable that so few, or so it would appear, see it this way or realize what are the repercussions for almost every aspect of Christian life, corporate or individual, of the way in which we construe the God-Christ relation. Accordingly I now draw attention to an incisive analysis of the christological problem, which sets out to show just how much the fabric of Christian life, belief, behavior, liturgical practice and worship, is structured around two poles, belief in God and belief in Christ. In a book entitled *God or Christ?* (trans. John Bowden from *Dieu ou le Christ*, London: SCM Press, 1981), Abbé Jean Milet looks at this bi-polarity not from the standpoint of theology or philosophy but of social psychology. The theologian or Christian philosopher would find Milet's title misleading. Surely at no time in Christian history has a rigid dichotomy been set up between God and Jesus Christ: only on the gnostic heretical fringe was a sharp distinction drawn between the God of the Bible, that is, the Old Testament, Creator of the material world (which the gnostics took to be inherently evil), and the Christ, or true, essential divine spirit, which came to dwell in Jesus and left him at his death.

As a social psychologist, however, Milet is not in pursuit of a viable theory in the abstract of the God-Jesus relation. If he were, I believe it would follow the lines of traditional Trinitarian doctrine. What he has in mind rather is the idea that the dynamic of Christian faith and life has resided from the outset *in the inner tension within the believer's existence* between theocentricity and christocentricity. He describes the tension as a sort of tug-of-war in the Christian psyche between the utmost reverence for the all holy and majestic God, who can be venerated only from afar, and the strong sense of the closeness of Jesus as a brother who once shared our human condition to the full. So long as, from a psychological and social perspective, we focus on Christian *experience*, then the very essence of Christianity lies in the magnetism exerted by the two poles: the

God who is the end of all our living, and the Christ who is the open door toward that end. To seek escape from the two-way pull and to move exclusively in the direction of one pole or the other is to diminish authentic Christianity to the vanishing point. Milet's chief interest is in the existential effects or consequences of leanings or tendencies within the Christian fold toward the Godward side or toward the Christ side. He provides a very useful account of how the different sensibilities inspired on the one hand by theocentricity and on the other by christocentricity affect personal, social, and religious attitudes and behavior in the Christian community (he has Catholicism especially in view).

Two examples only may be cited. The first concerns the manner in which we conceive of the religious institution. The God-centered perspective, with its stress on God the Father Almighty, evokes the image of the Christian faithful as subordinates, as in the earthly household, where, in patriarchal contexts at least, the father holds sway. It requires no great wit to see how this links up with the reverential designation of the pope as "Holy Father," and how in turn it goes with a "high" view of the church as a hierarchical institution, in which, so to speak, authority is passed down through the ranks. By contrast the Christ-centered perspective, turning in upon Jesus and observing the lowly character of his ministry and his disapproval of an authoritarian religious establishment, encourages desacralization of the institution, and envisages authority in the church not as a power hierarchically transmitted, but as a charisma comparable to, if not identical with, Jesus' own charisma.[1]

Our second example from Milet bears a resemblance to the first. It relates to the way in which the polarities peculiar to Christianity condition political and social thought and action. The theocentric outlook, with its orientation toward the Father God who ordains all the powers that are and imposes good order over all, is strongly disposed to a paternalistic conception of authority and supports a monarchical system of government or a regime in which supreme power is vested in an overlord: witness the exalted position of the emperor in the Holy Roman Empire or of the feudal lord in the Middle Ages. The God-centered perspective has always fostered a conservative spirit and a strong hostility to any departure from the status quo in a firmly established and well ordered society. By comparison, where a Christ-centered perspective prevails, there is a more delicate sensitivity to the image of Jesus Christ the brother. His pronouncements in the Beatitudes constitute a reversal of authoritarian norms or regulations and of the hierarchical ordering of things: "Blessed are the poor in spirit"; "Blessed are the peacemakers"; "Blessed are those who suffer persecution for the sake of justice." So the idea of superior and inferior, master and servant is suppressed and yields to the dream of an egalitarian society and of a universal brotherhood and sisterhood. If this assessment is correct, would not the theology of liberation that has become so prominent of late in Latin America, and elsewhere as well, be more appropriately called the *Christology* of liberation, since Jesus is normally envisaged as a revolutionary hero.[2] Milet, I dare say, has possibly too rigidly compartmentalized the theocentric and christocentric inspiration and their respective effects at the social psychological level.

Nevertheless his main points are well taken, nowhere more so than in his long line of argumentation that in the modern period it is christocentricity that has triumphed with the self-same consequences for social and political life we have just been describing. Imagining Jesus as the radical protester against the power structures of society and the violence used to maintain them, the Christian must more than anything else fight for justice and equality. As to the religious life, the image of Jesus as "spokesman of the people, especially the poor" has built up a picture of the priest as above all "the poor Jesus-man," celebrating the Mass in the vernacular and inviting participation in it as no more than a popular fellowship meal for all classes.[3] Whereas Milet's arguments here refer specifically to what has been happening on the Catholic front, he is well aware of the tremendous influence of the historicism that ensued from the Enlightenment and the resultant preoccupation in the sphere of liberal Protestantism with reconstruction of the life of the man Jesus.

Milet maintains, and it would be hard to refute him on this, that one of the most extreme forms of christocentricity has been the entirely Jesus-centered atheism of the God-is-dead movement — profoundly influenced also, to be sure, by the humanistic or materialistic philosophies of Ludwig Feuerbach or Karl Marx and the doom-laden nihilism of Nietzsche. Champions of the death of God turned the searchlight only on Jesus and saw him in his God-forsaken nakedness, shall we say, as the model fall guy, the man for others, the tragic hero, the archetypal revolutionary, and so on.[4]

Now none of the contributors to this book would countenance for a moment the God-is-dead ideology or the reduction of Christianity merely to a form of humanism. At the same time it is noteworthy that, in what they have written here at any rate, there is a dearth of reference to the Godward side of the bipolarity we have been considering. A likely reason for that is that we too share the sensibilities aroused by the christocentric inspiration and would concur in the widely influential view of such contemporary theologians as Hans Küng, Edward Schillebeeckx, and John Macquarrie, to name but three, that Christology must begin not from above with God in high heaven, but from below with the man Jesus, who lived and died in Palestine during the prefecture of Pontius Pilate around 30 C.E.

It is quite possible to begin Christology from below with the historical person Jesus of Nazareth without surrendering to an excessive christocentricity or the extreme Jesus-centeredness of those heralds of the death of God who not only excommunicated God from their own discourse about Jesus, but from his universe. Genuine Christian spirituality finds in Jesus the "reflection" of God. If we eliminate the direct Godward-orientation of Jesus' life or the altogether crucial place occupied by the language of the kingdom *of God* in his message, then we are left not with the Jesus of the Gospels at all, but with the figure of an avant-garde modernity too deeply colored, we repeat, by materialist or humanist philosophies that have been dominant of late.

There is, therefore, much to be said for Milet's contention that, for the sake of its future vitality and spiritual enrichment, the church must be geared up toward a renewal of the sense of the divine transcendence (with Jesus still seen, of course, as the medium of God's dealings with his world). Nonetheless there will be many, I fancy, who cannot go along with his advocacy of a revival of metaphysical rumination and mystical contemplation as the best way ahead.

It has not been possible here to describe or handle critically in detail the wealth of materials by which Milet supports his arguments. I have introduced his work because of its intrinsic importance and also because it is congenial to my own position in two principal respects. First it points up the high importance of a reverent theocentricity for balanced Christian life, faith, and worship, and to that extent corroborates our feeling that the *theological* dimension of the New Testament has suffered neglect. Neglect not only from scholars but from contemporary evangelists, whose preaching is concentrated on the redeeming God and scarcely at all on the *God of Creation*, with the consequent loss in their hearers of a sense of mystery, awe, and wonder. Our experience has been that in many worship services in American churches, an opening prayer of *adoration* has often been conspicuously lacking. Yet the prayer Jesus himself set before his disciples begins with the words: "Our Father *who art in heaven.*" Now, second, Milet's social psychological approach to the study of Christology means that he is not intent upon defining or refining Christian doctrine, but upon seeking to analyze behavioral patterns and social logics. He thus ensures, while sacrificing nothing of scholarly integrity, that Christology is brought down from the rarefied air of academic theorizing and is *earthed*, as it were, in the lives of people. This accords well with my choice of the rather worldly word "business" in reference to Christology (see below).

So far we have sketched out a broad landscape against which the essays that follow may be viewed. We can now go on to alert the reader in advance to some outstanding features of their content. The test case, or one of the frequently applied test cases in regard to the christological question, is discussion of the resurrection or the Easter texts of the New Testament. That the movement that eventually came to be called the Christian movement could not possibly have arisen without Easter is an irrefutable truth. But so very much hinges on how we understand "Easter." Orthodoxy has always insisted that nothing could conceivably explain the birth of faith in Christ's divinity or the transformation it effected in the disciples' lives except the actuality of an unprecedented physical occurrence by which Christ rose bodily from the grave and "appeared" to his followers (but the linking of "risen body" and "appearance" is very problematic, to say the least, when we consider the shape and form of the "appearance stories" in the Gospels!). Through the ages, however, theologians both orthodox and liberal (for many liberals too have defended the historical reality

of the resurrection as an isolable and singular event of the past)
have never found it easy to clarify, far less define, the nature of
the Easter "miracle." I say "miracle" mainly because the theologians we have in mind regularly take refuge in the notion
that what happened on the first Easter lies totally beyond our
ken. But in fact the normative mode of expression in the New
Testament is: "Christ was raised," which is equivalent to "God
raised him": so here we move across the frontier from any sort
of historical happening that could be empirically verified to the
realm of faith. Accordingly the "miracle" of Easter, if the term
is at all appropriate here, is *the birth or new-birth of faith*, initiated
not in the hyper-imaginative genius of the first disciples, but
by the staggering impact on them of the life and death of Jesus
of Nazareth. Willi Marxsen puts the matter succinctly: "Jesus is
risen simply means: today the crucified Jesus is calling us to believe."[5] In our judgment then the Easter reports of the Gospels
are best construed as giving moving expression in concrete narratives or stories to a new-found faith in God, which lives out of
ongoing or recurrent encounters with the crucified Christ. This
is the theme we shall be pursuing further in the later part of
our chapter.

As we turn now to the essays by Dr. James H. Charlesworth
and Dr. Leander E. Keck, titled respectively "The Righteous
Teacher and the Historical Jesus" and "Jesus and Judaism in
the New Testament," it should be noted that they exemplify
two different modes or facets of modern critical study of the
New Testament. Charlesworth operates primarily as historical
researcher into Jesus' life and life-situation. He investigates the
texts in order to get behind them, to recover and reconstruct the
facts about Jesus. Keck on the other hand examines the texts not
in order to reach out to something beyond them, but to discern
and explicate what later writers like Matthew, John, and Paul
were saying, years after Jesus' death, about his relation to Judaism. The two types of analysis are not the same, as Keck notes.
But neither are they in fundamental disagreement, for both are
essentially historical. If the critic is investigating the New Testament writings first and foremost as documents, which have
something to say rather than nothing or a specific point of view
to express, he or she is duty bound to explore fully the particular cultural influences that played upon each author. In the
case of the Pauline letters, for example, the critic simply cannot

avoid *historical* questions concerning the social, political, and religious circumstances that obtained in the immediate environment of the young Christian communities within the orbit of Paul's mission or missionary concern across the Mediterranean world in the first century C.E. But the interpreter of the writings, who wishes to let them say their own say in their own terms, is by no means necessarily hostile (most certainly not Dr. Keck!) to efforts to rediscover the facts about Jesus. He does not consider Jesus Research a waste of time, as not a few twentieth-century theologians have done. Rather in his influential work under the title *A Future for the Historical Jesus: The Place of Jesus in Preaching and Theology* (Nashville: Abingdon, 1971; rev. 2d ed. Philadelphia: Fortress Press, 1981) he argues eloquently and persuasively that Christian faith, life, and worship are inextricably bound up not with an inscrutable and impenetrable past event (the *Dass* of R. Bultmann), but with one we can *trust*, the man Jesus of Nazareth.

However, in the paper presented here, he sets out to show that those who choose to follow Jesus Christ do so not because they have garnered a fair amount of historical knowledge of the kind of person Jesus was or of what he said and did, but because of the interpretive framework in which this Jewish figure is located by the New Testament writers. Whatever precisely was Jesus' own attitude(s) to Judaism in the course of his ministry (a subject of animated debate), fairly radical shifts of perspective on Jesus' relationship to Judaism took place with the passing years of the first century C.E. Few will find fault with Keck's submissions: (1) Paul's primary concern was with gentile converts, who may perhaps have been associated with the Jewish synagogues of the Hellenistic Diaspora. In writing to gentiles, as the silence about it in his letters shows, he was not interested in locating Jesus in the Judaism of Jesus' own day. Instead the axis of Paul's theology is Jesus' cross and resurrection, and his task is to wrestle with their meaning for Israel, the Jewish people, who are the children *of his own time*. Paul asks, are the true children of Abraham (who in fact are the true Israel) the unbelieving Jews or all those who have said "yes" to the gospel of Jesus Christ? That the task involved much anguish of mind and soul for the apostle is graphically illustrated by Romans 9–11. (2) The dialectical tension, evident in Paul's situation, has largely been overcome in Matthew and John. The

stress in Matthew on Jesus' discontinuity with Judaism is not
so much a historical retrospect as a reflection of the widen-
ing gap between synagogue and church in the late first century.
In John that breach is complete: the Jews stand condemned by
their blind rejection of Christ, who has been rejected by and
has superseded the synagogue.

For Keck, therefore, if we want properly to comprehend the
meaning of Jesus Christ, we must stand *within the interpretive
framework* furnished by Matthew, John, or Paul, and at the same
time recognize that their respective interpretations can neither
be proved or disproved by historical-critical enquiry.

Now, whereas Charlesworth is an enthusiastic exponent of
what he terms "Jesus Research" (to distinguish it from earlier
quests of the historical Jesus), he would not, I think, quarrel with Keck's standpoint. In his important book *Jesus within
Judaism: New Light from Exciting Archaeological Discoveries,* his
large concluding section, "Jesus' Concept of God," makes that
quite plain: "Historians can prove that the cross is historical,
archaeologists may now be able to show us where he was crucified; but they cannot elicit a confession in a crucified Lord."
Or again: "Behind Christology lies no myth but an *interpreted
given*" (italics mine).[6]

Nevertheless his book turns for by far the greater part on
historical questions about Jesus and his life. This is the set purpose, of course, since he confesses that "he has edited out the
faith-oriented comments that are presently intrusive."[7] Through
his expertise in the Old Testament Pseudepigrapha, the Dead
Sea Scrolls, the Coptic Gnostic documents from Nag Hammadi
in Upper Egypt, and the most recent archaeological discoveries
in Palestine, he is able to shed fascinating light on the social,
political, and religious forces influencing Jesus in his words and
acts. It is when, in his book and in the essay published here, he
takes up the question of Jesus' self-understanding that he enters
an area of protracted and heated controversy.

In the present essay he takes up the Parable of the Wicked
Tenant Farmers (Mark 12:1–12, Matt. 21:33–46, Luke 20:9–19)
and undertakes a comparative study of Mark's version with a
passage relating to the Righteous Teacher of the Qumran Community (1QH 8.4–11), but principally with the extra-canonical
Gospel of Thomas 65. Such an exercise is in itself extremely
useful since it should remind many in the churches who are

unaware of it that exegesis and interpretation of the New Testament writings ought not to restrict their purview solely to these writings, but must turn for illumination to related extra-canonical documents. Moreover Charlesworth's study serves to show that even a considerably later version of a parable of Jesus may contain elements of tradition that go back further, and closer to Jesus himself, than earlier versions.

I share with Charlesworth what is now probably the consensus view, that the earlier part of the Parable of the Wicked Farmers most probably comes from the lips of Jesus. It does reflect the landholding conditions existing in Jesus' day, but not those after the Jewish revolt and the destruction of Jerusalem around 70 C.E. But I am not at all sure that verses 7–9 derive ultimately from Jesus. The conspiracy of the farmers to kill the heir so that they would inherit the vineyard (Mark 12:7) does not make much sense, since presumably the landlord would still be the owner of the vineyard on the death of the heir. Charlesworth argues that verse 8 ("they took him and killed him, and cast him out of the vineyard") must belong to a date within Jesus' own ministry, since it betrays ignorance of how Jesus was actually killed *outside of Jerusalem* (i.e., the vineyard). The argument is interesting, but unconvincing. The "and" (Greek *kai*) in "and cast him out of the vineyard," may well be epexegetic, that is, "they took him and killed him, *having cast him out of the vineyard*." In that case, verse 8 would be post-crucifixion and reflect the actual manner of Jesus' death. At all events, many scholars still hold that the titles "son" or "Son of God" are not Jesus' self-designation, but belong to the preaching or confessions of the early church.

But even if the conclusion of this parable could be taken as original to Jesus, and he did after all conceive of himself as "son," we might well ask, what then? Charlesworth, in his recent volume, discovers fifteen examples of the term "son" (as a messianic title) in the literature of Early Judaism and adduces from this that it could have been employed by Jesus and was not necessarily the creation of the church. But in the Jewish literature cited, the term is a functional one and alludes to God's *adoption* of Messiah as the one who would *act* as his final agent ("adoption" being a metaphor related to the notion of the "anointing" or "appointing" of a kingly figure). Accordingly we can readily agree with Charlesworth's statement that "certainly this was in no way in line with the physical sonship so prominent in the ancient Near East."[8] And to be sure, even if Jesus used it of himself after the Jewish fashion, it stands, as Charlesworth himself stresses (in chapter 2), at a very distant remove from the Trinitarian formulations and metaphysical speculations about the divine nature of Christ as the *only* "son" of God in the third and fourth centuries of the church's history. But what an exciting question, as raised by Charlesworth, is that of Jesus' self-understanding, even if we hold that there need not be an organic, one-to-one connection between what Jesus thought of himself and what the later church said about him!

We should remember that, despite recent advances in our awareness of the environment of Jesus and his place within it, as well as of the character of the Christian communities in the late first century C.E., these are still "gray areas," and our knowledge remains limited. We can, I think, justly say that without surrendering to excessive historical scepticism, like that of the German Form-critics vis-à-vis the historical Jesus. One of the distinct merits of Dr. Walter Weaver's scholarly contribution is that it strikes a fine balance between what we can know and what we do not know of the life of Jesus. His decision to structure his essay as an account of his own personal pilgrimage in Christology is to be applauded, since it lends to his treatment a dimension of existential urgency: here indeed is an essayist deeply involved with his subject. The reader might usefully compare Weaver's statements regarding Easter with those of Keck and myself. But what is truly impressive about Weaver's essay is the way in which his autobiographical approach enables him to set forth comprehensively the kaleidoscopic shifts of perspective that have occurred in the last three decades or so among both biblical scholars and theologians. Most of the big names are there — and linked incisively with the effects they have had on the perception of the Jesus question in us lesser mortals. The candor with which Weaver speaks of developments in his own attitude to and conception of the historical Jesus issue reminds me of a series of articles that appeared some years ago in the Scottish journal *The Expository Times* entitled "How My Mind Has Changed." No less preeminent a theologian than Karl Barth contributed to the series. In this, at least, if in no other sense, can ordinary members of the churches resemble the great theological giants of the century: the prerogative to change our mind belongs to us just by being human. In the Christian context, the ever unchanged or unchanging mind is a barrier to the maturation of Christian character and renders men and women fit only for the milk of the Word of God and not its solid food (1 Cor. 3:2).

Possibly the most arresting and suggestive part of Weaver's presentation is his closing exposition of the idea that a fruitful way to construe the relation of Jesus to the Christ of the church's preaching is to think of Jesus the "parabler" as, after his death, become God's Parable in the minds and hearts of his followers. Jesus' parable-language in the course of his ministry exposes for "those who have ears to hear" the presence, in the midst of the ordinary stuff of life, of a God, a totally unexpected God, who does not play the game according to our human rules (see, for instance, the Parable of the Laborers in the Vineyard, Matt. 20:1–14), but shatters our regular norms and standards. The deeds of Jesus also can be regarded as *acted* parables, in complete harmony with his spoken parables, his life of servanthood, his table-fellowship with sinners, his befriending of the outcasts and the dispossessed. Behind these deeds stands a God who, as we would state it, comes upon us quietly and takes us by surprise. But above all the shameful death of Jesus on the cross perfectly matches the lowly, sacrificial, or cruciform (Weaver) quality of his life. The sight of the strange man hanging on his cross becomes the Parable of God for those who have the eyes of discernment.

Where Weaver has employed the idea of *parable*, in my essay I have referred to the *mythopoetic* framework in which the story of Jesus' life and death is encased in the reports of the Gospels. I am conscious of the fact, however, that in recent theological discussion the word "myth" has become a very slippery one indeed, used in a variety of senses, often without exact definition; and besides it is grievously misunderstood by church people. It may be then that "parable" is to be preferred, although the reader may observe that we both arrive, terminology notwithstanding, at approximately the same theological viewpoint. At any rate, it is to be hoped that Dr. Weaver will take the Jesus-the-parabler-become-the-Parable-of-God idea further in future writing.

But we must now let the following essays speak for themselves and conclude by reemphasizing the point previously made. Years ago an Anglican scholar-bishop affirmed that what the churches need most are believers who dare to inquire and inquirers who dare to believe.

NOTES

1. J. Milet, *God or Christ?* trans. J. Bowden (London: SCM Press, 1981), 58–61.

2. Ibid., 72–74.

3. Ibid., 177–80.

4. Ibid., 193–97.

5. W. Marxsen, *The Resurrection of Jesus of Nazareth,* trans. Margaret Kohl (London: SCM Press, 1970), 128.

6. J. H. Charlesworth, *Jesus within Judaism,* Anchor Bible Reference Library (New York: Doubleday, 1988), 156.

7. Ibid., xi.

8. Ibid., 152.

Chapter 1

Jesus as Parable

Walter P. Weaver

With the indulgence of my colleagues, I would like to depart from the usual scholarly format. I want instead to outline a story — my own — consistent with the ultimate goal of coming to speak about the theological task as a parabolic one.

A NARRATIVE APPROACH

I do not quite recall just when my theological awakening began; while still an undergraduate I first encountered the historical-critical study of the Bible, which came to me as revelation and, indeed, as deliverance. For already I had questions in my head about the text. I had not, however, anywhere in church been given the freedom and encouragement to pursue an inquiry into the biblical text, much less to do so methodically. So I welcomed that exposure; I think it had a great deal to do with my final determination to pursue the teaching vocation.

In seminary I solidified my decision to go on to doctoral work, especially in the field of New Testament. One person instrumental in that determination also contributes to this volume, Prof. Hugh Anderson.[1] It was he who first stirred my interests in New Testament and in particular introduced me to the figure of Rudolf Bultmann, who would become my most influential theological mentor.[2]

From graduate studies I went on to teaching. I do not need to rehearse all those years. But in that time the interest originally generated by historical criticism increasingly focused on the significance of critical method in relationship to faith. It is probable that my exposure again to undergraduates facilitated that concern. It was apparent that undergraduate students were less appreciative of historical method than I had been. And as the impact of the fundamentalist movement began to show up among entering students, my awareness of the problematic nature of the historical method for students grew. The problem was expressed for me in the question of the historical Jesus, for it is there that the whole issue comes most pressingly to the surface, at least within the context of Christian faith.

DEFINITION OF THE PROBLEM

Let me now turn briefly to a definition of the problem, as it presented itself to me and as I have wrestled with it since. Further, let me confine the definition to the question of the historical Jesus.

We learn from critical study that the Jesus whom we knew from our youth, whom we perhaps first met in Sunday School, has become to us a stranger. That Jesus once so familiar — who calmed the waters, walked the sea, raised the dead, imperiously claiming to be the Son of God-Son of Man — this Jesus never had any existence. The Jesus of history (who may in reality be stranger still) has come to dwell in his stead. This Jesus is hard to know; little of him remains from the visitations of the scholars and critics. We are left with a shrunken Jesus, and inevitably the question must rise whether this laborious penetration behind the kerygmatic picture is worthful. How can it serve the interests of faith? Or can it at all? Or does anyone care whether it does?

The problem with the historical Jesus is then that we have here an order of knowledge that cannot seemingly be assimilated into faith. To know Jesus historically is one level of understanding; to know him faith-fully is another level, and the two do not appear to most persons to belong together.

It was self-evident to me, if not to my students, that historical study of Jesus would not go away, and indeed should not. The birth of the modern historical consciousness in the Enlightenment period was a momentous event in the West; the right to apply the fruits of that mode of thinking to the biblical text was purchased at great price. To be asked to abandon that was tantamount to renouncing one's birthright in the modern world, so it seemed to many of my generation. Faithfulness to Jesus surely must not mean loss of responsibility for that world.

I set out to probe various possible resolutions of this problem. It bothered my theological sensibility to be a participant in a process whose consequences were either devastating for traditional faith or at best were poorly thought out.

IN QUEST OF SOLUTIONS: BULTMANN

I extended my theological vision in a variety of directions. I was confident of two things: I could not go back to some pre-critical period — the Jesus of history was unavoidable — and I wished to remain identifiably within the Christian tradition.

Bultmann's views have been so widely discussed that I need not rehearse them in any systematic way, and space does not permit that in any case. Bultmann was himself raised in the liberal theology of nineteenth-century Germany; and the concerns of that school can still be seen in his program: the need to address scientific "modern man," the demythologizing project, the retention of critical method along with a posture of faith.

Yet he found it necessary to turn away from that liberal heritage in order to preserve the faith-character of Christian faith. In reality, Bultmann continued the gap between the Jesus of history and the Christ of faith that emanated from liberalism, only he opted for the kerygmatic Christ.[3] The Jesus of history appeared to Bultmann to be a dead-end, not only because so little can be known, but because faith itself cannot be linked to such a historically contingent event. At least, the uncertainty of historical knowledge must not be confused with the decision-character of faith. Hence Bultmann was content to allow the separation between faith and historical research to stand. "Faith cannot be dependent on the results of historical research" became a kind of stereotypical truism in dialectical theology. It is a theme actually found in many quarters, perhaps nowhere more eloquently articulated than by Martin Kähler.[4]

So Bultmann solved the problem of conflict between criticism and faith by separating the two rather sharply. Faith has the character of a decision; it is related only tangentially to any particular set of historical facts. In the case of Christian faith, all that is required to be known about Jesus is the mere facticity of his appearance in history (the famous *Dass*). And, of course, since faith itself is couched in mythological terms, it has to undergo demythologizing in order to be presented as a real possibility in a non-mythological world.[5]

I also soon learned that if I wished to party with Bultmann, I had to dance with Martin Heidegger. For when the Easter kerygma is demythologized, it has to translate into something, and this "something" was found *zuhanden* by Bultmann in the historicity of human existence as set out in Heidegger's analysis of the *existentialia* of *Dasein*. So I discovered how to speak of such things as "care" and "thrownness," of "fallenness" and of authenticity and inauthenticity, of resolve to being-unto-death, and much more. Various forays into *Sein und Zeit*[6] proved to be forbidding, however, and it always seemed to me that the New Testament itself was easier to deal with.[7] Yet the conversation with Heidegger proved useful, in that the ground was prepared for what came to be thought of as the post-Bultmannian movement.

Now there is much about Bultmann that I have retained and for which I am continuously grateful. Yet in the end I had to abandon his path, because, on the one hand, I could not go along with his conclusion that faith is immune from the consequences of criticism or is isolated from them; and, on the other hand, I also found, as many have, his individualization of the Christian message to be too constricting. To comment only on the first: to come to know the Jesus of history may not, as Bultmann insisted, affect that decision about the kerygma. But certainly it does have some consequences for the content of faith, i.e., for the image of Jesus that one subsequently carries about with oneself. It is a little like growing up and discovering that your parents are human; it does not affect your evaluation of them, but it alters your mental picture of them.

I am well aware of the dangers of criticizing Bultmann; as Barth pointed out,[8] one should be careful throwing stones at Bultmann, lest one strike Luther. And certainly Bultmann's entire program is to be seen as his own brilliant construal of the doctrine of justification by faith (alone). At the same time I never felt that everything must give account of itself to the Law-Gospel dialectic. That is probably my Methodist background showing itself.

Now there is one point at which I think Bultmann's position remains unassailable. Ultimately, for him the issue comes down to what one makes of the Easter faith. It is in that "event" that the proclaimer became the proclaimed, that Christian faith first arose, that Jesus became the Christ. The Easter faith cannot be read back into the "life" of Jesus, lest one should render it superfluous. To do so also implies a distortion in the Trinity: Jesus as the Christ is made present only in the kerygma, which is to say, faith is the work of the Spirit through the act of proclamation. If such faith can simply be read off the events of history, then the Spirit becomes unnecessary.[9]

Of course, it is also the case that "Easter" is itself a non-verifiable event. The only "event" available to the historian is the rise of faith in the disciples. So we have a non-verifiable event giving rise to a non-verifiable faith. In Bultmann's view that is good, for it guarantees the immunity of faith. Faith never can have any props, including those of provable facts, if it wishes to remain faith. Here the ghost of Kierkegaard is hovering about.

The historical Jesus then remains for Bultmann simply a phenomenon of history. Whatever interest one may have in that Jesus is not the interest of faith. It is an interest that may affect one's self-understanding as historian, not as Christian. In other words, history always casts up various possibilities for understanding oneself, whether the self-understanding represented by Socrates or Napoleon, by Lincoln or someone else. Anyone is free to investigate these possibilities, to seek a *geschichtlich* encounter with a figure of history as a possibility for understanding oneself. That was what Bultmann's 1926 book on Jesus was about, so he said. But such a historical inquiry is not kerygma.[10]

Now I think that the argument about the inaccessibility of Easter must be conceded. I do think there is more to be said than Bultmann has allowed, and I wish to sketch that out a bit later. But the main point still stands, so it seems to me, that is, that something occurred there that is more than renewal of the Jesus before Easter (which would only be resuscitation) and that was transformative. This "something" probably will always remain enigmatic to us; not even the New Testament is so bold as to attempt to explain that. For this reason also I found Wolfhart Pannenberg's historical "proof" of resurrection to be stretching the limits of critical method; and, in any event, his argument seemed to end up merely proving that "resurrection" is possible only for those whose theological horizons are apocalyptic — something that has become rather problematic today.[11]

To introduce Pannenberg brings me to a little reflection on some other of my mentors. I mentioned already the post-Bultmannians, represented especially by Gerhard Ebeling and Ernst Fuchs. This movement among Bultmann's students, called the New Hermeneutic, was concerned with some problems thought not well attended to in Bultmann's program. For example, while the demythologizing proposal was a hermeneutical project, it presupposed a certain view of language that was inadequate. In fact, for Bultmann statements are basically of two sorts: assertive and existential. Though the statements of the New Testament intend to be the latter, they appear to be the former and thus need to be demythologized. Bultmann is averse to language as assertion or predication, for it objectifies God.

But Bultmann's view of language was thought to be deficient. There is more to be said, and the New Hermeneutic leaned upon the so-called "later" Heidegger, who turned increasingly — in his quest for Being — to the *existential* of language as the mode where Being discloses itself. In other words, language is not just an arbitrary system of signs and symbols, but is the repository of the disclosedness of Being, the "house of being," as Heidegger said, and humankind is its shepherd. Hence language, or at least primordial discourse (not just everyday language, which is generally mere "prattle"), is constitutive of existence; the historicity of existence has been exchanged for the linguisticality of existence.[12]

Now both Ebeling and Fuchs take up this insistence on the importance of language and apply it to the New Testament. There is recorded the "word-event" (Ebeling: *Wortgeschehen;* Fuchs: *Sprachereignis*) that is Jesus, including the historical Jesus. (Word-event is understood, following the "later" Heidegger, as a unity of event and the language it calls forth). Fuchs has especially directed attention to the parables of Jesus as such language-events, whereby God is brought to expression (comes into language). Additionally, Fuchs has emphasized that the context of Jesus' word is his deed, i.e., the parables must be seen as bound to Jesus' own acts (word-events).[13]

Ebeling has in particular addressed the question of the place of critical method, granting that it has a necessary "clearing" function,[14] and he has also, along with Fuchs, put the historical Jesus at the center of Christian faith. Indeed, Jesus is the "text" of faith; he is the language-event that creates faith. Or Ebeling can say that Jesus was the witness of faith who became the basis of faith. Faith is what came to expression in Jesus.[15] There is no playing off of historical Jesus over against Christ of faith. Both are taken up into the theological enterprise. History is taken up as "language event," while faith continues to be understood as a structure of existence.

All that seemed promising and directed itself to many of my concerns. The insights into the nature of language are surely important; parable, for example, is a particularly conspicuous instance of non-objectifying speaking, to which Heidegger's view of primordial discourse seemed to lend itself so well.

At the same time not everything was comfortable. Many of Bultmann's apparent shortcomings were simply continued, such as the reduction of eschatology to the moment of decision and the compression of faith to individualism. I also felt uncomfortable at being clasped so closely to the bosom of Heidegger, about which already Hans Jonas had warned.[16]

So it seemed to me that what had really happened in the New Hermeneutic, at least vis-à-vis Bultmann, was that the "proof of God from existence"[17] had been replaced by a proof of God from language, which simply carried with it the more subtle shift from "saving event" (Bultmann) to "language event" (Ebeling, Fuchs). In addition, I found it ironic that a theological effort anxious to ensure the movement from text to sermon was itself so obscure that few could really participate. So I hoped that there was a better way.

I made yet another visitation into systematics — always dangerous for a mere historian — and consulted one of the other great theological minds of our time, Paul Tillich. I found views similar to those generally prevailing in Neo-orthodoxy (dialectical theology), with a highly interesting variation. Tillich, like Bultmann, concedes the full use of historical criticism, even labels the employment of it "an expression of Protestant courage"[18] in that Protestantism undertook a serious risk by subjecting its own Scriptures to critical scrutiny. At the same time what is important for Tillich is not the historical Jesus, about whom little can be known, but the biblical picture of Jesus which has the power to evoke faith and hence to communicate the "new Being." Whether or indeed how much of this picture corresponds to actual history, i.e., is rooted in the historical Jesus (otherwise: in actual events of history), is ultimately not significant for Tillich. What matters is the picture itself, as symbol, and its capacity to vivify the power of the new Being.[19]

That, too, is extremely attractive. It certainly convinced Van Harvey, for example, whose work *The Historian and the Believer*[20] I greatly admired, and still do. But at length Harvey came to side with Tillich, concluding that, in the last analysis, it is not theologically important to link the biblical picture of Christ to the historical Jesus. All that matters is the power of the picture to awaken faith.[21]

Yet there was something about this solution that bothered me. For one thing, it seemed, reminiscent of Bultmann, to render historical work on the text insignificant theologically. Of course, the historian's labor does not have to be significant theologically, but I found it impossible to exist schizophrenically. More important, the loosing of the biblical picture of Christ from its moorings in Jesus entirely generated a sense of unease, for it seemed to leave me defenseless against any and all claims to truth. Are all pictures to be valued according to their capacity to awaken faith? What picture and whose faith? In any event, in these days of clever picture-makers, we had best beware of where our blessings go.

Certainly it is true that christological statements cannot be limited to what Jesus said about himself or thought about himself, even if we could know that.[22] But then the question arises as to what does give warrant to make christological statements. The Easter faith alone? Current Christian experience? Appeal to the Spirit? Would we not then have to renew the Pauline struggle at Corinth all over? Are christological statements really entirely to be divorced from what we do, in fact, know about Jesus? Could they, for example, freely contradict Jesus? I am only asking, as opposed to implying that I somehow know exactly how the answer should go; but in any case, whoever thinks that it does not matter what Jesus himself said on the subject ought to try that out on a group of undergraduates or lay people in the church.

So once more I found myself backing away because someone had concluded that my work as historian was essentially irrelevant. And that just did not somehow seem to fit into my calculus.

I also spent some literary time with the newer generation of thinkers, such as Jürgen Moltmann,[23] who began his novel program with an effort to make fruitful the rediscovery of eschatology around the turn of the century. He was undoubtedly correct that none of the major theological figures of the twentieth century had really succeeded in unlocking that discovery, for reasons we cannot here rehearse. Moltmann proposed to rethink *theology as eschatology*, i.e., to exploit the eschatological symbols in a systematic way, in terms of promise and hope. Along with that — indeed, out of it — went a relevant political theology.

Moltmann has not been particularly concerned with the problems posed by historical-critical method. Naturally the resurrection is central in his program, but, unlike Pannenberg, he did not propose to establish its probability historically. In fact, he argued that it was to be regarded as an "event" without analogy, to be assumed as the basis for a view of history different from that prevailing in the use of historical criticism. The resurrection is not a part of some history, the history of death, but itself makes history and opens up the future. Moltmann's early thought was rather iconoclastic, and his method was to contend for the faith against other modern options. I must confess that I never really found much help for myself there, given the nature of the problem I was wrestling with. I found Moltmann, though exceedingly brilliant, to be unclear with regard to what was really to be expected from this Novum, this future promised in the resurrection. It is also the case that his project has moved on from his initial work, especially developing around the doctrine of the Trinity as the central motif in theology.[24]

I crossed the paths of many others, delving into what might be called "God-problem" theologies. Among them were Langdon Gilkey,[25] Schubert Ogden,[26] William Hamilton,[27] Thomas Altizer,[28] and Paul van Buren.[29] I even looked at such thinkers as R. G. Collingwood,[30] whose thought about historiography was helpful, if not directly illuminative for my concern. Later I found the Catholic theologians Hans Küng[31] and Edward Schillebeeckx[32] to be extraordinarily insightful; their reproductions of the state of scholarship on the question of the historical Jesus were superb. Schillebeeckx especially has some splendid analysis of criticism and its consequences for faith.[33] Yet neither quite provided the solution for which I was looking. Perhaps there was no such solution, as often seems to be the case in theological matters.

Nevertheless, I began to form some conclusions of my own, which I wish now to share. They led to an answer with which I thought I could live.

SOME TENTATIVE CONCLUSIONS

My thinking on these issues congealed into the following theses.

1. We cannot have the Christ of faith apart from the historical Jesus (understood as the historian's Jesus). Critical method is our fate, as much a part of our world as the automobile or telephone. It cannot be abandoned and its rights must be fully conceded, i.e., there can be no arbitrary limits set on its use. This conclusion has some obvious implications for the teaching and preaching functions of the church. Preaching, for example, has to be kept honest when it comes to texts dealing with Jesus; one ought not to abuse such texts historically.[34]

2. We cannot have the historical Jesus apart from the kerygmatic Christ. There can be no setting of the two theologically over against one another.[35]

The historical Jesus alone is inadequate to deal with the monumental problems that face us, and in some sense have always faced us. I do not mean only the urgent issues of nuclear war and the like, but the perennial matters of human identity and the threat to meaning. It is clearly the case, for example, that the ancient problem of theodicy, of how the righteousness of God can prevail in the world and in our lives, simply cannot be met by appealing to the Jesus of history. Mark at least seems to agree, when he pictures the earthly Jesus dying with just that question on his lips. The question cannot be *answered* under any circumstance, but it can at least be taken up and resolved in the mode of hope, given in the Easter experience. Strictly speaking, however, that experience involves more than the historical Jesus.

3. There is a continuity between the Jesus of history and the Christ of faith. This was the concern of the so-called "New Quest" of the historical Jesus and its main point was well taken. As a historical observation, the kerygma cannot be derived *from* the message of Jesus, but neither does it *contradict* the message of Jesus. Analyzed existentially, Jesus' own teaching in the parables and sayings of the kingdom proclaims the same understanding of existence as Paul's notion of justification on the basis of grace alone. Of course, a Bultmannian might object that such existence can only be obtained in the proclamation of the kerygma, implying that clinging to the historical Jesus leaves one still under the Law, but that seems to be out-Luthering Luther. Easter was transformative for Jesus, in that it "translated" him into eschatological existence; such a transformation was necessary for Jesus if I am to have the experience of grace through Jesus. But having arrived there, it may be that I can also have that experience by looking back through Easter to the Jesus of history.

4. We can therefore appeal to the historical Jesus primarily as a theological strategy for our time, i.e., on the basis that Jesus, the entire picture of this Jesus related by historical reconstruction, provides a Parable that can form the basis of meaningful existence.

I need to explicate that in some more detail.

Let me take the first part, appealing to the historical Jesus as a theological strategy for our time. I understand our time to be still a secular one; the phenomenon described by persons such as Bonhoeffer remains a reality. I do not think that the recent pentecostal movement forms an exception. Whether it is also to be characterized as a movement of the Spirit in our times is not for me to say, but to some extent it would appear at least to be a comment on the banality of much religious practice in the mainline churches. I would think that, in any case, like most such movements it will make its peace with the mainstream culture and some of its impetus will be swallowed up. I do not intend thereby to dismiss its significance, but neither would I wish to overstate the case.

I am not quite as convinced as Bultmann seemed to be that our contemporary, Western human being is to be approached as strictly a scientific creature. He or she is that, to be sure (or at least implicitly agrees to the scientific "world"), and scientific method obviously has a profound impact not to be undervalued. At the same time this modern being remains open to other possibilities, or else religion as such would simply perish. He or she very likely must still appreciate that there are other forms of discourse than the scientific one and that these other forms provide an equal access to the truth about existence.[36] He or she likely does not need to be taught about the relativity of truth, for that is already assumed. But that sense of relativity enhances the possibility of speaking to contemporary persons a parable, a historical parable, for it is accompanied by the relativity of all historical learning, and it also comes under the strictures of historical method. It may therefore be less likely to be taken with hostility, or even dismissed as a "myth," as can happen with the traditional kerygma. At least as Parable it has a historical referent, just the thing which is often suspected to be lacking in "myth."[37]

Now as to the second part — that Jesus, the historian's Jesus, be construed as Parable, and that this Parable can in some way be made the basis of meaningful existence — this part rests on some assumptions about the nature of parable and how it functions in language. I can only briefly indicate the contours of this thought.

It is widely conceded today that parable is essentially a metaphor.[38] Metaphorical speaking is the basis of our communicating, from the more mundane even to the most esoteric scientific formulations. To take the first level: If, for example, I hear a student say, "Wow! Look at that fox," I know that the person using this expression does not intend to describe claws on the end of someone's fingers or long hair covering on the body, but rather is referring to the sexual appeal of some other person. Or, to take a scientific instance, the notion of "hole flow" in electron theory certainly is metaphorical; literally, it makes nonsense, but metaphorically it expresses "something like" what is happening and makes possible an operational view of the nature of reality. It is probably fair to say, as a generalization, that the entire field of sub-nuclear physics would be hard put to get along without metaphor, or (what is metaphorically based) models.[39] Similarly, Jesus himself used metaphor, in the form of parable, to speak of what cannot be spoken of in merely discursive or conceptual speech. Parable was his most characteristic way of speaking about the unspeakable.

To be more specific, the parables of Jesus may be said to have these characteristics:

a. *Everydayness.* They are astonishingly "secular," in that they describe rather ordinary, mundane situations. The purpose of that is to allow the hearer to "get in gear" with the story, to identify with the situation.

b. *A "hooker."* A hooker is an unexpected something, an element of reversal or surprise. This part tantalizes or stirs the listener to thought or response. It may even have a shattering effect, causing the hearer to reorient his or her world, or at least be faced with that possibility.

c. *Openendedness.* Parables do not moralize or allegorize. They are truly open and leave something to be decided. In short, they summon up worlds and expect the hearer to decide whether he or she can participate in or make the leap from his or her world to the world of the parable.[40]

Now back to my thesis.

It is theologically proper to think of Jesus as Parable for the following reasons.

1. As already indicated, parable was the most characteristic mode of his own self-expression. It epitomized his way of thinking and speaking.

2. The secularity of the Parable corresponds to the secularity of the world, a world where today God-talk is difficult.[41] The Parable presents the possibility of speaking secularly about the transcendent.

3. Jesus as Parable gets us beyond the problem posed by historical-critical method. On the one hand, it preserves the full rights of the historian, whose work is here allowed to come into the circle of the theological enterprise; on the other hand, faith retains its investment as well, for still one must make a decision about the significance of the Jesus story. Like a good parable, that story remains openended, because (1) the end of the Parable, the crucifixion, poses a question about Jesus; (2) history itself leaves open the question of whether the Jesus of history has yet any future; and (3) the future itself leaves unanswered

the question of whether the future of Jesus is bound up with the future of the world (the eschatological question).

•

Now there are questions of all sorts that arise from this line of thought, but I cannot enter into them here. What I wish to do instead is to indicate where others have thought along similar lines and then to attempt a brief characterization of what it might mean to indwell the Parable that is the historical Jesus.

At about the time I was thinking in terms of Jesus as Parable, there appeared the work by one of the contributors to this volume, Prof. Leander Keck, entitled, *A Future for the Historical Jesus: The Place of Jesus in Preaching and Theology*.[42] I was delighted by this work, for it, too, sought to make a place for the historian's Jesus within faith, emphasizing how just that Jesus could be presented as the one to be trusted for salvation. The elucidation of "trust" and "salvation" was extremely helpful, the full accreditation of the historical method was exciting, and, finally, there was also the suggestion that just this Jesus was to be regarded as a "Parable of God" in the totality of his words and deeds.

I obviously had no quarrel with any of that, except that I chose not to use the language of "trust" and "salvation" with regard to the historical Jesus. Those terms appeared to me to have limited linguistic cash value when utilized with regard to a figure of history. And when it was further said that this Jesus was trustworthy because of the resurrection, then it became a bit more problematic as to whether we were any longer talking about the historical Jesus.

Still, Keck's work remained at an evocative level and did not extend its reflection to working through the implications of thinking of Jesus as Parable. Perhaps there was nothing more to be said, but I needed to find that out for myself.

Here and there were also others who had utilized the idea of Jesus as Parable; it gets noticed in John Dominic Crossan,[43] in Schillebeeckx,[44] and more especially is treated by John Donahue.[45] But nowhere is there any effort to work out the implications.

There also appeared various works by Sallie McFague, in a series of three books over the period 1975 to 1987. The first of these was *Speaking in Parables: A Study in Metaphor and Theology*,[46] followed by *Metaphorical Theology: Models of God in Religious Language*,[47] and a third along the same line, *Models of God: Theology for an Ecological, Nuclear Age*.[48] McFague sets out to do theology in a minor key, so to speak, i.e., not systematically, but as narrative, as metaphor. She takes her cues from the parables of Jesus and from Jesus as parable, as the basis for constructing new models (sets of metaphors) of God in our time. She is primarily pursuing a feminist agenda in seeking to overturn the patriarchal models of God and to find newer, more appropriate ones.

I am particularly sympathetic to the notion that theology ought to be modest in its speech, or, as I would put it, parabolic. I also have no special interest in system making, though I certainly raise no objection to those who do. We ought also to recognize that the traditional models of God are time-and-culture bound in ways that are felt as oppression by some groups. In McFague's third volume the feminist critique of patriarchy has hardened: the patriarchal models of God are seen as destructive (hierarchical, depriving persons of freedom), threatening to the life of the world (giving rise to militarism and lack of care of the earth). What she attempts to do, based on three major strands in the parables of Jesus and Jesus as parable of God (his parabolic speech, his table fellowship with the outcasts, and his death on the cross), is to translate these elements into current models that will offer the possibility of re-imaging the relationship of God and world in a new and salvific way. The ways attempted are God as mother, lover, and friend, and the world as the body of God. It is a bold program, full of imagination, and does indeed contain the "shock" value of a good parable, forcing a rethinking of the old "world." I find it to be provocative and in many ways persuasive.

At the same time McFague's agenda is not my own, and neither is she concerned with examining the problematic of historical-critical method for faith. Jesus as Parable of God functions heuristically for her, apparently, as entrée to the theological task, but is not the content of the task. From her side, of course, it would be asked whether what I had in mind should be labeled theology at all.[49]

So I still find myself thinking about what it might mean

to hold to the historical Jesus as Parable. How would it look to dwell in that kind of world?

Let me briefly sketch some of the contours of a parabolic world.

THE SHAPE OF A PARABOLIC WORLD

It would be appropriate to set out how I see the picture of the historical Jesus that forms the content of the Parable, but obviously I cannot do that here.[50] I will content myself with at least some things that seem to me to be characteristic elements in Jesus as Parable.

1. *Identity with the dispossessed.* Jesus cannot be claimed to support the rich and powerful over against the poor and oppressed. This is such a pervasive element in the Jesus-Parable that it is virtually the ruling principle. While knowledge about Jesus' activity is modest, there is sufficient information to show that there was a remarkable degree of coherence in the totality of his work. Three strands make up this coherence: his proclamation of the kingdom (good news to the down-and-out), his teaching on the *agape* that does not calculate worthfulness, and his typical behavior in associating with, even having table fellowship with the unworthies ("sinners and tax collectors"). Radical grace as reversal of normal expectations characterizes all three. It also unites his eschatology and his ethics.

There are obviously implications of a great variety in this observation. It follows that certain kinds of activity become parabolic, such as political events, for it is there that the concern for the dispossessed becomes critical. Community is also inherent in the Parable, though surely the community of parable-people is indeed an odd one: an eschatological community of the dispossessed, characterized by its *agape*-style and its acceptance of all sorts of unacceptables.[51]

2. *True life as cruciform.* A fourth strand could be added to the above three: the crucifixion. One of the great puzzles of Jesus' life has always been determining how he regarded his end, his death (discounting the passion predictions, which look like Easter experiences projected backward). I do not think we can know the answer to that, but I think we can say that the crucifixion represented a certain logical end to his activity. To

be crucified was to be put among the dispossessed and, according to Jesus' own words and deeds, that was where he belonged. To be killed in just that way was, in the context of first-century Judaism, a humiliating death, cut off from God (as Paul knows; cf. Gal. 3:13; Deut. 21:23). It could be said that if Jesus' "life" had ended with his dying in bed of old age, the Easter faith itself could not have been called forth. The contradiction between his "life" and his death would have been insurmountable. Crucifixion was the "logical" outcome of his life.[52] For my part I believe that Jesus understood that very well. If the cry from the cross is authentic, it likely expresses the pain and isolation that nevertheless accompany such a savage separation from life.

This cruciform quality runs throughout the picture of Jesus' words and activity. It takes the shape of a servant-existence, the finding of life in its giving, the abandonment of pretensions to goodness, the discovery of grace where others hear only law and judgment. Here also occurs again that reversal that runs in parables generally, for the commendation of such an existence moves contrary to the ways of the world. The notion that the universe operates on the side of the slaves is generally abhorrent these days, and very hard to sell anywhere. Perhaps it can be embodied only in parabolic worlds, empowered by the humiliating end of Jesus himself.

3. *God as parabolic.* It is not possible to appeal to the Jesus of history and ignore the God-question, as though Jesus were merely self-recommending. Jesus without God is a contradiction. Yet the Parable does not authorize limitless talk about the transcendent. One clue here is Jesus' own unique speech pattern in addressing God as *Abba.* I find the sense of that to lie not so much in intimacy as in modesty, in restraint based on the recognition that all our talk to and about God is like that of children just learning to speak. It is better not to overspeak.

And the God about whom and to whom we are to speak does not fit our systems anyway. This God never shows up on command, nor performs at our direction. And when He or She does appear, it is always unremittingly cruciform. That is the parabolic God, and perhaps such a God, too, will not be as popular as the miracle-doer so widely sought these days in certain popular and religious circles.

4. *Eschatological hope.* That Jesus himself was an eschatological preacher has been a given in New Testament studies

the better part of a century. To what extent Jesus clung to imminence in his expectation is less certain.[53] In any event, was
chronological time all that important to Jesus? And even if
it was, that would not invalidate the Parable, but only show
that Jesus perhaps had in common a little more with the
apocalyptists of his time than many would wish to allow (a
foreshortened sense of time).[54]

But I do not think it is possible to appeal to the Parable that
is Jesus and bypass the eschatology. That would redo some of
the ways of old style liberalism, which sought to ally itself with
the "ethic" of Jesus while remaining largely silent on the eschatology or dismissing it as simply a culturally conditioned
thought form. And while it may not be possible or even desirable to function in the state of eschatological intensity, there
remains the necessity for hope and for the ultimate prevailing
of the rule of God. Without such hope, without the confidence
that the universe harbors benevolence, there would be no reason
to turn to the Parable that is Jesus.

To think of hope is also to have in mind the resurrection of
Jesus himself. For the most part critics have little to say about
"resurrection."[55] And while we surely cannot gainsay the fact
that "resurrection" as such is beyond the historian's inspection,
yet it is a strange historical method that remains completely
silent about that which assured the survival of the historical
Jesus. Jesus after all did achieve something (in a manner of
speaking), a community worshiping in his name, so that, from
one perspective, it can be said that one of the effects of Jesus'
"life" was this eschatological movement that survived him.

"Resurrection-language" is a particular form of speech, out
of the apocalyptic tradition, to express an inexpressible experience. And though I must agree that as historian I have no direct
access to whatever gave rise to that mode of discourse, I do
nevertheless think that we can say something about the lines
running between the pre- and post-Easter pictures of Jesus, and
the gist of it seems to me to be about as follows.

Consider again the inner coherence of the Jesus-story: he
proclaimed the rule of God for the disinherited, he associated with the "dead," he commended the *agape* that does
not calculate worth. As the logical outcome of such a "life,"
Jesus' cross-death then concentrated the meaning of his "life"
as cruciform. Crucifixion was literally the only appropriate

summarizing symbol for Jesus. Whether the disciples comprehended this fact is uncertain; I suspect that they had some
inkling and were unable to persist in the face of it, fleeing back
to Galilee. The cross was then catalytic in a broad sense.

Probably also in Galilee Peter's experience, the root experience of "appearance," also occurred. In that experience —
whether in an ecstatic moment accompanied by audition and/or
visualization is unknown — Peter laid hold of the basic structure of Jesus, the reversal structure of parable itself. It might
better be said that the structure laid hold of him, and I would
not quarrel with that. To go one step further, then, we have to
say that this Easter experience, which grasps or is grasped by
the reversal structure, is itself the most radical reversal of all.
It itself expresses, "Out of death, life." The appearance experience of Peter means that he was seized by the Parable-structure
and set in motion by it. Whether that occurred in an ecstatic
moment cannot be known. It could be added that, if the tradition of Peter's own reversed-cross death is to be admitted, then
it can be said that Peter demonstrated that he had really gotten
the point.

I suggest, then, that "Easter" in some sense belongs to the
story, the story precisely of the historical Jesus. Of course, there
is very much more that might be said by way of implication, but
the details must remain for a future day.

NOTES

1. There is still a great deal of profit in his book *Jesus and
Christian Origins* (New York: Oxford University Press, 1964).

2. I would have gladly learned from Karl Barth, but I found a
minimum of concern with the matter there. Criticism, for Barth, has a
kind of preliminary function and makes way for the genuine understanding that occurs only in the reproduction within oneself of the
theological *Sache* of the text. Of course, the early Barth was intent on
recovering something for Christian faith that had gone astray in the
culture Protestantism of his day.

Naturally I have had many other outstanding teachers, most notably Howard Clark Kee, whose excellence in scholarship needs no
presentation from me.

3. The liberal focus on the Jesus of history was, after all, polem-
ical, as Schweitzer pointed out. The Jesus of history had been enlisted

in the campaign against orthodoxy and in the service of raising up a new, more scientific Christianity.

4. *The So-Called Historical Jesus and the Historic Biblical Christ*, trans. Carl E. Braaten (Philadelphia: Fortress Press, 1964; published originally 1896).

5. The demythologizing essay is found in Hans Werner Bartsch, ed., *Kerygma and Myth: A Theological Debate*, trans. Reginald Fuller (New York: Harper, 1961).

6. ET, *Being and Time*, trans. John Macquarrie and Edward Robinson (New York: Harper, 1962).

7. Bultmann's "translation" seemed to work really well in the case of something like the Pauline anthropology — the heart of the matter for him anyway — but its utility was not so self-evident elsewhere.

8. In Hans-Werner Bartsch, ed., *Kerygma and Myth: A Theological Debate*, trans. Reginald H. Fuller (London: SPCK, 1962), 2:123.

9. I take it that this assumption underlies much of what Bultmann had to say in his reply to the "New Quest," in *The Historical Jesus and the Kerygmatic Christ: Essays on the New Quest of the Historical Jesus*, trans. and ed. Carl E. Braaten and Roy A. Harrisville (New York: Abingdon Press, 1964); see especially the end of Bultmann's essay, p. 42.

10. ET, *Jesus and the Word*, trans. Louise Pettibone Smith and Erminie Huntress Lantero (New York: Charles Scribner's Sons, 1934; new ed., 1958). The relevant statements of Bultmann are found in *Kerygma and Myth*, 1:117.

11. Pannenberg's original argument appeared in his work *Jesus-God and Man*, trans. Lewis L. Wilkins and Duane A. Priebe (Philadelphia: Westminster Press, 1968).

12. Still the best overview is James M. Robinson and John B. Cobb, Jr., eds., *the New Hermeneutic* (New York: Harper, 1964).

13. See Fuchs's work in *Studies of the Historical Jesus*, trans. Andrew Scobie (Naperville, Ill.: Alec R. Allenson, 1964).

14. See Ebeling's works in *Word and Faith*, trans. James W. Leitch (Philadelphia: Fortress Press, 1963), especially the first essay; also see *The Problem of Historicity in the Church and its Proclamation*, trans. Grover Foley (Philadelphia: Fortress Press, 1967); and *Theology and Proclamation*, trans. John Riches (Philadelphia: Fortress Press, 1966). The analogy to the early Barth is self evident; this confluence between early Barth and later Heidegger could lead one such as Heinrich Ott to attempt on that basis a reconciliation between Barthian and Bultmannian perspectives. Cf. *The Later Heidegger and Theology*, ed. James M. Robinson and John B. Cobb, Jr., New Frontiers in Theology 1 (New York: Harper, 1963).

15. *The Nature of Faith*, trans. Ronald Gregor Smith (Philadelphia: Muhlenberg Press, 1961).

16. In his address at the second Drew Consultation entitled, "Heidegger and Theology," later published in *The Phenomenon of Life* (New York: Harper, 1966). Jonas warned that Heidegger's philosophy never provided any basis for distinguishing between the divine and the demonic, i.e., the call of Being must simply be answered. Language as response to such a call leaves no ground for resisting the summons of evil. Jonas cited Heidegger's own early endorsement of Hitler's summons to the youth of Germany to follow his nationalistic vision.

17. The phrase is that of Jürgen Moltmann, *Theology of Hope*, trans. James W. Leitch (New York: Harper, 1967), 62.

18. *Systematic Theology* (Chicago: University of Chicago Press, 1957), 2:107.

19. Ibid., especially the whole discussion on pp. 97–118. Tillich did suggest that there was an *analogia imaginis* or analogy between the picture which arouses faith and the historical reality. He also argued that faith can guarantee its own foundation, i.e., that the picture has the power to produce faith, but this capability cannot be guaranteed to relate to the historical factuality of Jesus of Nazareth. See the statement in *Dynamics of Faith* (New York: Harper, 1957), 88, that faith can attest to the saving power of the picture of Jesus which produced it (faith), "no matter how much or how little can be traced to the historical figure who is called Jesus of Nazareth."

My colleague at Florida Southern College, Dean of the College, Ben Wade, himself a Tillich expert, has advised me that I am misreading Tillich here, who would certainly not wish to deny the historical ground of faith in Jesus. At least my company is fairly good; see Van Harvey, in n. 21.

20. Van Harvey, *The Historian and the Believer* (New York: Macmillan, 1966). Harvey's work remains probably the best analysis of the "morality of knowledge" involved in what the historian does.

21. Harvey acknowledged his conversion in an essay, "A Christology for Barabbases," *Perkins Journal* 29 (1976): 11. In his original work he had maintained the necessity for the link with the historical Jesus, at least in the form of a "perspectival image" of Jesus that had survived in the record.

22. E.g., Leander E. Keck, "Toward the Renewal of New Testament Christology, *New Testament Studies* 32 (1986): 372–73. The same point was made somewhat more forcefully in an earlier essay, "The Historical Jesus and Christology," *Perkins Journal* 29 (1976): 23.

23. *Theology of Hope*; see my n. 17.

24. The argument is found in *Theology of Hope*, especially chap. 3. See also the programmatic essay in Frederick Herzog, ed., *The Future*

of Hope (New York: Herder & Herder, 1970). The major outlines of the trinitarian thought are found already in *The Crucified God: The Cross of Christ as the Foundation and Criticism of Christian Theology,* trans. R. A. Wilson and John Bowden (New York: Harper, 1974).

My colleague W. Waite Willis, Jr., in his significant work *Theism, Atheism, and the Doctrine of the Trinity* (Atlanta: Scholars Press, 1987), argues that the trinitarian views of Barth and Moltmann provide a successful means of addressing "protest atheism," i.e., the atheism founded on the failure of traditional theism to speak to the theodicy question. The trinitarianism of Barth and Moltmann opens up new possibilities, since it provides a sensuous epistemology (as Feuerbach demanded) — the concrete event of Jesus of Nazareth — and since human suffering is taken up into the immanent trinity and is a part of God himself. The argument is rather more complex than I can here indicate and makes its case persuasively. At the same time it is obviously not the kind of thing that would have a very siren effect on an old fossil like myself, who disdains even the task of systematics and thinks that God-talk ought to be restrained. Such a thought would seem incredible to someone like Barth, who after all wrote endlessly on the subject. Of course, he then confessed that he had really said nothing. In any event, clever as is the union of Barth and Moltmann in the service of apologetics, in the end one still has to ask whether this trinitarianism has the power to change anything. One might hope that persons are more moved by it to do something about the injustice and misery of the world. That, of course, would be highly significant in itself. But perhaps also the rehearsing of the Parable can have effect as well.

25. *Naming the Whirlwind: The Renewal of God-Language* (Indianapolis and New York: Bobbs-Merrill, 1969).

26. *The Reality of God* (New York: Harper, 1966). The way was prepared in his earlier work, *Christ without Myth* (New York: Harper, 1961).

27. His general views at that time were available in Thomas J. J. Altizer and William Hamilton, *Radical Theology and the Death of God* (Indianapolis and New York: Bobbs-Merrill, 1966).

28. *The Gospel of Christian Atheism* (Philadelphia: Westminster Press, 1966).

29. *The Secular Meaning of the Gospel* (New York: Macmillan, 1963).

30. *The Idea of History* (New York: Oxford University Press, 1956).

31. *On Being a Christian,* trans. Edward Quinn (New York: Doubleday, 1976). Available also as an abridged version in "Pocket Books" (New York: Simon & Schuster, 1978).

32. *Jesus: An Experiment in Christology,* trans. Hubert Hoskins (New York: Crossroad, 1981).

33. Ibid., especially the discussion in chap. 1, 44–88. Schille-beeckx makes the point that while criticism cannot lay a ground for faith, it nevertheless is crucial in providing the content of faith, i.e., it keeps faith from becoming an abstraction or devotion to an idea. I think that is a valid and useful point.

34. Theologically, the least that can be said for the historical Jesus is that he keeps the kerygma from entering prematurely into glory. This is not an unimportant point today, when so much of popular Christian piety seems bent on arriving already at the kingdom.

35. So also recently Eduard Schweizer, *Jesus Christ: The Man from Nazareth and the Exalted Lord,* ed. Hulitt Gloer (Macon, Ga.: Mercer University Press, 1987), especially 12ff. Schweizer emphasizes beginning with the Easter kerygma, but also that the earthly Jesus is the "criterion of all faith" (12), and wishes to include the crucifixion and Easter encounter within this picture. In short, he intends to relate kerygma and historical Jesus in the closest possible way, going beyond what most historians would find comfortable.

36. I would wish, for example, to agree with the notion that the avenues to the truth of our existence provided through art, music, great literature, drama, and related activities are just as important as that evidenced in scientific method. A scientific description of two persons making love, for instance, would doubtless absolutely beggar the mind for mundaneness, yet no one (at least of my acquaintance) would question the truthfulness of that human experience as something acutely *essential* to being human or doubt that it was better told by Shakespeare in, say, *Romeo and Juliet.*

37. Post-modern and/or post-liberal constructions do not, as far as I can see, obviate the continued reading of the secularity of the world as reality to be dealt with. For a helpful discussion of how such views, including a deconstructionist one, might relate themselves, if at all, to the influential work of John Dominic Crossan, see the essay by Sheila Greeve Davaney, "A Historicist Model for Theology," in the recent *Jesus and Faith: a Conversation on the Work of John Dominic Crossan,* ed. Jeffrey Carlson and Robert A. Ludwig (Maryknoll, N.Y.: Orbis Books, 1994). It is at the same time also apparent that not everyone would be comfortable with my continuing to characterize society generally as content with the relativity of truth claims. The post-liberal view that truth claims are to be adjudicated within traditioned communities is self-evidently a useful one for the Christian community, but it remains less clear how such communities carry on their discourse with other truth-claiming communities.

38. There are good summaries in the works of Sallie McFague mentioned in this article. See also Robert W. Funk, *Language, Herme-*

neutic, and *Word of God: The Problem of Language in the New Testament and Contemporary Theology* (New York: Harper, 1966); idem, *Parables and Presence* (Philadelphia: Fortress Press, 1982); John Dominic Crossan, *Cliffs of Fall: Paradox and Polyvalence in the Parables of Jesus* (New York: Seabury Press, 1980); Paul Ricoeur, *The Rule of Metaphor: Multidisciplinary Studies of the Creation of Meaning in Language,* trans. Robert Czerny with Kathleen McLaughlin and John Costello (Toronto: University of Toronto Press, 1977); idem, *Essays on Biblical Interpretation,* ed. with intro. by Lewis Mudge (Philadelphia: Fortress Press, 1980).

39. A good discussion of various literary types and especially their use in scientific thinking is Ian G. Barbour, *Myths, Models and Paradigms: A Comparative Study in Science and Religion* (New York: Harper, 1974).

40. Structuralists also point out certain other constant features, such as the "law of three" (three illustrative characters) or, according to the Greimas model, six actants (presence of six events or persons or elements in a typical narrative parable). I must confess that, while all these analyses may well be instructive, I have not been terribly excited by structuralism. Especially I find its a-historical stance to be a putoff. There may indeed be "deep structures" of the mind that can be illuminated by the type of literary analysis represented in structuralism, but I am in no position to judge. I see some possibilities for understanding the power of the Jesus story along those lines, but I would not have the slightest idea as to how such a notion could be integrated with what is already known about the electro-chemical functioning of the brain.

The issues involved in the structuralist analysis of parables are well represented in *Semeia* 1 (1974) and *Semeia* 2 (1974). See also Funk, *Parables and Presence.*

41. By the difficulty of God-talk, I do not mean the absence of such discourse in our world, where surely there already is an abundance of such. Indeed, the abundance — as might be seen among the television religious figures, for example — seems only to point to the problem: How to make meaningful God-discourse in a society where such talk seems to many to lack any discernible reference, on the one hand, and, on the other, in a society where the most conspicuous God-speakers seem to be the least credentialed and often most arbitrary and sometimes socially retrogressive figures.

42. Nashville: Abingdon, 1971; rev. 2d. ed. Philadelphia: Fortress Press, 1981.

43. Crossan, *Cliffs of Fall,* 14.

44. *Jesus: An Experiment in Christology,* 158–59.

45. "Jesus as the Parable of God in the Gospel of Mark," *Interpreting the Gospels,* ed. Luther Mays (Philadelphia: Fortress Press,

1981), 148–67. Donahue's concern in this piece was to show how Mark presents Jesus as a "parable of God." He did so by utilizing the elements in C. H. Dodd's definition of parable and correlating those with motifs in Mark's picture. I have no problem with that, but it is obviously of a different order of concern from my own. Now also there is the work *The Gospel in Parable: Metaphor, Narrative, and Theology in the Synoptic Gospels* (Philadelphia: Fortress Press, 1988), which extends that line to the whole synoptic tradition.

46. Philadelphia: Fortress Press, 1975.

47. Philadelphia: Fortress Press, 1975.

48. Philadelphia: Fortress Press, 1987.

49. I have less concern with undertaking the "thought experiment" with new models, preferring instead to allow the text to make its own transition into the contemporary setting. Of course, the effort at translating is a commendable one, and certainly McFague's is both novel and imaginative.

It is worth noting, with regard to all these mentioned works, that I would prefer not to say what the Parable is "of," in keeping with the openendedness of a parable. Surely the historical Jesus is in some sense transparent to the God-question, but let us not anticipate that, any more than his parables did. The picture of Jesus could also be thought of equally well as "Parable of humankind."

50. There would doubtless be some differences from someone else's picture, and everyone knows well the story documented by Schweitzer of the seemingly infinite variety in the depictions of the historical Jesus. I do not downplay those variations, but neither should they be overdrawn. There are also large areas of agreement these days. In any case, this variation not merely attests to the relativity of all historical reconstruction, but also points to the power of the Parable to present itself in amazing degrees of perspective. It is as though the Jesus story were a kind of prism through which one sees the refractions of one's own existence, perhaps of all human existence. Somewhere in that possibility lies the secret of the power of the Jesus story.

The documentation of the continuing quest for Jesus in the twentieth century is a project to which I am committed as this essay goes into reissue. This story, which will be told in three volumes, will initially cover primarily the English-language concern with the historical Jesus in the time known in German-language studies as the time of "no quest." I am currently at work on this volume, while the remaining two volumes, to be authored by Ernst Baasland of Oslo and James Charlesworth of Princeton, will flesh out the series as the end of the century, indeed the millennium, approaches. The series will be published by Trinity Press International.

51. Here too could be seen the healing tradition, as good news to the desperate and helpless.

52. Jürgen Moltmann argues powerfully (*The Crucified God*, esp. 145–53) that Jesus died a "godforsaken" death, with a sense of being totally abandoned by God. Jesus' death was problematic precisely because it was the death of that one who had proclaimed the gracious, near God experienced as the Father, that Jesus had counted on just this God to demonstrate God's kingdom, but had instead died crying out in despair. This death has then to be understood theologically as an issue between Jesus and his father, between Father and Son, i.e., as an issue to be grasped only from a trinitarian perspective. (It points toward a suffering within the very being of God.)

It would seem that, for Moltmann, Jesus' death radically contradicted his "life" (explicitly on p. 162) and that this contradiction can be resolved as a problem only within the Trinity. I have instead suggested that Jesus likely understood the logic of his own activity, that his "messy" death nevertheless was understandable in the human terms of terrible agony. That Jesus cried out for God in Moltmann's sense seems to imply that his life ended in a meaningless disappointment that his expectation was not fulfilled. That would be pressing these modest texts, which first speak the Markan perspective, to rather broad limits. One is also reminded of Schweitzer's Jesus, who "threw himself on the wheel of history," which rolled on and crushed him. Only Schweitzer had no interest in working out the trinitarian implications.

It could be further said that my point revolves around the mode of Jesus' death, while any mode would theoretically do for Moltmann — death by stoning, perhaps — as long as Jesus faced it with a sense of abandonment by God. From this perspective the resurrection appears as a kind of "salvage operation," rather than, as I would suppose, a vindication of life-as-cruciform. But the Easter faith did not surmount a contradiction; it sustained an interpretation. Of course, it did so by being itself a "demonstration" in power of the permanency of the reversal structure and therefore also moved Jesus into eschatological existence.

It could also be asked, "If Jesus recognized the logic of his own activity, in what sense then is the Easter faith really a reversal?" Certainly not, I would guess, of his expectations, but just as certainly of those of the people around him, including perhaps even the disciples — probably even them at first, and then in the broadest sense the whole world.

I suspect that the main difference between Moltmann and myself on this point is that I am not sanguine about what can be deduced regarding Jesus' expectations from these texts in Mark. On the other hand, it is clear enough that to be subjected to crucifixion was, in the context of Judaism, tantamount to being accursed by God and therefore cut off from him. Did Jesus realize that? I do not know, but I imagine that he was aware of the logic of his activity, as I have already indicated. Moltmann might make his case (which is rather crucial for the theological position he evolves) on the ground that crucifixion itself amounted to being considered cut off from God, and that Jesus himself experienced that.

53. E. P. Sanders (*Jesus and Judaism* [Philadelphia: Fortress Press, 1985]) sets Jesus solidly in the context of Jewish restoration eschatology, as a Theudas-like eschatological figure who expected the imminent kingdom, accompanied by the new temple, with himself as king and the disciples who followed him as regnant with him. Sanders seems to be inheriting Schweitzer's mantle, not only in the eschatological emphasis, but in seeking for the connection in Jesus' "life" as well. It is a splendid work, though what I miss in it is any really serious engagement with the parables of Jesus.

The degree to which Jesus may be considered as holding to an imminent expectation is subject to considerable debate these days. For a judicious analysis, see the essay by Marcus Borg, "Jesus and Eschatology: a Reassessment," in the volume co-edited by James Charlesworth and myself, *Images of Jesus Today,* Faith and Scholarship Colloquies 3 (Valley Forge, Pa.: Trinity Press International, 1994).

The striking work of John Dominic Crossan (*The Historical Jesus: The Life of a Mediterranean Jewish Peasant* [San Francisco: Harper, 1992]) also declines to attribute imminence to Jesus. Crossan's work, controversial as usual, likely will set the agenda for Jesus-debate for some time to come (see already the work *Jesus and Faith: A Conversation on the Work of John Dominic Crossan,* referred to in my n. 37). The contribution of John Meier (*A Marginal Jew: Rethinking the Historical Jesus,* Anchor Bible Reference Library [New York: Doubleday, 1991]) awaits the appearance of volume 2, though clearly Meier's work is one that will compete in its thoroughness and sophistication for equal attention. Crossan has especially engaged the methodological issues with novelty and power.

54. I do not see a great deal in common between Jesus and those apocalyptists whose writings have survived, including some in the New Testament. What often separates them is twofold: (1) a massive shrinking in Jesus' words of the bizarre symbols and calculations — a virtual "demythologizing" — and (2) the apocalyptist's devotion to the Law and the concurrent conviction that only the righteous by the Law will survive in the eschaton. That assumption seriously breaches Jesus' proclamation of good news to the undeserving.

55. Bultmann remains the purest exemplar. His book on Jesus ends without a word even about the resurrection *faith.*

Chapter 2

The Righteous Teacher
and the Historical Jesus

James H. Charlesworth

Conferences in Poland, England, the United States, Israel, and elsewhere have been convened to celebrate the fortieth anniversary of the discovery of the Dead Sea Scrolls. Specialists on Early Judaism and Christian origins recognize the sensational significance of these texts, which provide startling new information on pre-70 Palestinian Judaism.

For those of us who are Christians this vast, still undigested data is of special importance; it enables us to view better the Judaisms that were current when Jesus lived and taught. Today there is a consensus that the Dead Sea Scrolls have revolutionized our study of the first and contiguous centuries. For our present purposes that means we now read the documents in the New Testament in a more informed and critical way. Through documents actually held and copied while Jesus was alive we are drawn closer to events contemporaneous with him.

The purpose of this essay is to compare the apparent self-understandings of the founder of the Dead Sea Scroll Community, the Righteous Teacher, with the founder of the Palestinian Jesus Movement, Jesus of Nazareth. Our present dual focus will be upon a psalm that probably reflects the Righteous Teacher's self-understanding and a parable that most likely contains a glimpse into Jesus' self-understanding.

THE RIGHTEOUS TEACHER

Forty years of work on over a hundred scrolls and fragments of others plus archaeological work on Khirbet Qumran and the Qumran caves have produced the following widely recognized portrait of the Righteous Teacher. He had been an influential priest in the Jerusalem Temple. Some leading scholars conclude that he had served as high priest. While this possibility should be admitted, it is certain that he and his group were the legitimate heirs to the high priesthood. They claimed, probably correctly, that they were the descendants of Zadok or true Levites. Due to a major rift among rival priestly groups he eventually was forced out of the Temple. Sometime around the middle of the second century B.C.E. he led a small band of followers into the Judaean wilderness. In the wilderness they eventually found the ruins of an old fortress that clearly, as archaeologists have shown, predates the Babylonian captivity of the sixth century B.C.E. The small band of priests rebuilt the fortress and turned it into a "monastery." Subsequently they were harassed by the rival and illegitimate priests in the Temple cult.

Two calendars were used, a lunar one by the Jerusalem priests and a solar one by the Qumran priests. It is possible that on the Day of Atonement, when the Righteous Teacher and his group were dedicated to religious observances, "the Wicked Priest" invaded their sacred halls. He may well have severely injured the Righteous Teacher.

The death of the founder of this community must have shaken his followers, because they held firmly to the belief that God would soon vindicate them; but we have no record of their reflections on his death. They certainly did not believe that he would return to them, and it remains unclear whether they held to a belief in the resurrection of the individual after death. This idea was, of course, already well known in Early Judaism, as we know from studying the Books of Enoch, Daniel, 1 and 2 Maccabees, and many other Jewish works.

Sometime around the year 100 B.C.E. the community was

greatly expanded, as we know assuredly from the archaeological excavations of Qumran and of Cave IV. Other Jews
obviously joined the community, since it is highly probable that
the Qumran Covenanters were a celibate group of priests.

THE SELF-UNDERSTANDING
OF THE RIGHTEOUS TEACHER

What did the Righteous Teacher think about his exile and his
place in the history of God's salvation? How could he find
meaning in a wasteland, far removed from the center of the
Holy Land, and the House of God's own dwelling? What was
the purpose of his priestly lineage? Was there any hope for him
and his faithful few? Where was God? Had he given up on
his wayward people? These questions are ours, but surely he,
as a brilliant, highly educated, and dedicated Jew, must have
raised and pondered similar issues. But is there any evidence
of what he was thinking, and what he really thought about
himself?

Since the first-discovered Dead Sea Scrolls were published,
distinguished scholars have claimed that the Righteous Teacher
wrote all of the *Rule of the Community,* the *Thanksgiving Hymns;*
later experts even claimed that he wrote the *Temple Scroll.* These
scrolls cannot be attributed to the same person; each of them is
a composite of traditions that come from different periods. It is
equally unlikely that the founder of the community wrote no
portion of the extant scrolls; he was well trained and founded
a community that above all is distinguished from other Jewish
groups by the quantity of documents it copied and composed.

The special hymnbook of the Qumran community is the
Thanksgiving Hymns, or *Hodayoth.* Along with numerous other
scholars I have concluded that some of the hymns were composed by the Righteous Teacher. As Professor Gerd Jeremias
has shown, in these hymns we sometimes find the use of the
first person singular that is distinct and represents a specific individual.[1] The most impressive example of a psalm composed
by the Righteous Teacher is in the *Thanksgiving Hymns,* in column 8 (1QH 8.4–11). Here is my idiomatic translation of this
allegorical and autobiographical psalm:

4. I [praise you, O Lord, because you][2] placed me
    as an overflowing fountain in a desert,[3]
    and (as) a spring of water in a dry land,[4]
5.   and (as) the irrigator[5] of *[6] the garden.[7]
    You [have plant]ed a planting of cypress, and elm,
    with cedar together[8] for your glory;
6.   (these are) the trees of * life, hidden[9]
    among all the trees of the water,[10]
    beside the mysterious water source.[11]
    And they caused to sprout the shoot[12]
    for the eternal planting.
7. Before they shall cause (it) to sprout they strike root,
    then send forth their roots to the river (*ywbl*).
    And its trunk shall be open to the living water;
8.   and it shall become the eternal fountain.
    But upon the shoot (*nṣr*)
    every [beast] of the forest shall feed.
    And its trunk (shall become) a place of trampling
9.   for all those who pass * over the way (*drk*).[13]
    And its branches (shall be)[14] for every winged bird.
    And all the tre[es] of the water
    shall exalt themselves over it,
    because they shall become magnified in their planting.[15]
10. But they shall not send forth a root to the river (*ywbl*).[16]
    And he who causes to sprout[17] the hol[y] shoot (*nṣr*)
    for the planting of truth is concealed
11. with the result that he is not * esteemed,
    and the sealing of his mystery is not perceived.[18]

This is a remarkable psalm. It is not only composed by the Righteous Teacher; it also reflects his own self-understanding. He praises God for planting him "as an overflowing fountain in a desert." He does not bewail the loss of his high position in the Temple cult. He acknowledges that he is in the desert (on a marl terrace overlooking the Dead Sea). But he celebrates his followers. They are "the trees of life" that are unrecognized and uncelebrated, because they are "hidden among all the trees of the water." He, the Righteous Teacher, is the "irrigator of the garden" and "the mysterious source."

Most importantly, the present does not disclose a ground for either lamenting or rejoicing. All meaning comes from the perspective of the culmination of the divine drama. The Righteous Teacher's followers are the ones who are preparing —

indeed are — "the eternal fountain," the "garden," and "the eternal planting." The future of God's promises is grounded on the present actions of the founder of this community. The faith of the Righteous Teacher is firm. His self-understanding as the Irrigator of the Eternal Planting is allegorically expressed in this psalm.

There is more. The suffering of the Righteous Teacher and his followers is also represented in these lines. He portrays himself as the Irrigator of the garden that will produce the shoot for the eternal planting. But the "shoot" has endured much suffering: the beasts feed on him; he has become "a place of trampling." The other priests, "the tre[es] of the water" have exalted "themselves over" him, "because they have become magnified in their planting." These phrases refer to the wicked priests who are in an exalted position in the Temple cult. Again, the Righteous Teacher refers to himself as one who is "concealed," "not esteemed," and "not perceived." Yet, he is convinced that he is the one who has been chosen by God to cause "to sprout the hol[y] shoot for the planting of truth," that is the eternal garden that will surpasss in the Endtime the paradisiacal state of the Garden of Eden.

One of the remarkable achievements of forty years of research on the Dead Sea Scrolls and Early Judaism is the ability to see behind this allegory some history of the Dead Sea Scroll Community, and even some self-understanding of its founder. Clearly, the Righteous Teacher is convinced that through him God is producing the eternal planting of truth. His teaching — his interpretation of the prophets and the Torah — is the water that sustains the garden; he is the Irrigator. Unfortunately, the historian is forced to point to another example of a devout person who had false hopes.

THE HISTORICAL JESUS

Two hundred years of searching for the historical Jesus have illustrated one perennial tendency. Authors portray Jesus in terms of their own ideals, customs, and dreams. In *Das Leben Jesu* (Tübingen, 1835, 1836) D. F. Strauss, a German pantheist, portrayed Jesus in light of Hegelian dialectics. In *La Vie de Jésus* (Paris, 1863) E. Renan gave us a romantic Jesus with a

French flair. In *The Divine Propagandist* (London, 1962) L. Beaver-brook, an expert in mass media, describes Jesus as a ruth-lessly efficient orator who mastered the art of personal example and propaganda. In *The Black Messiah* (New York, 1968, 1969) A. B. Cleage, Jr., a black clergyman, portrays Jesus as one who struggled for the disenfranchised and would have favored black power.

If we wish to avoid creating Jesus in our own image, we must be self-critical. If we are to learn anything about the Jesus of history, we must not read our own ideals into that time long ago and far away. We must struggle to live in Pales-tine before the burning of the Temple in C.E. 70; then we will certainly realize that we are strangers in that ancient Semitic environment.

Jesus wrote nothing, except — perhaps — for the word, words, or symbols that he allegedly wrote in the sand, ac-cording to John 7:53–8:11 (which is an apocryphal expansion). His earliest followers are never portrayed as scribes who wrote down for us his teachings.

It is apparent that Jesus' authentic words were altered significantly in roughly the forty years that separated his cru-cifixion from the composition of the first Gospel. It is equally certain that Jesus' followers were enthusiastically possessed by the conviction and experience that Jesus had been raised from the dead by God. They were also obviously interested in the Jesus they had known earlier; and they always identified the risen Christ with the one they had known previously in Galilee and Jerusalem. In the last ten years scholars have shown far more confidence than their former teachers in knowing some-thing about the pre-Easter Jew called Jesus.[19] This confidence is due not only to refined methodology but also to an enlightened perception of pre-70 Palestinian Judaism, thanks to the fruitful work on the Dead Sea Scrolls and other Jewish writings.

The following portrait of Jesus seems now to be widely accepted by many New Testament specialists. Jesus had some relationship with John the Baptist, who certainly baptized him. He began his public ministry in or near Capernaum and called men and women to follow him. He did select a special group, the twelve.[20] He performed healings and probably also ex-orcisms. He was an itinerant preacher who proclaimed the nearness (even presence at times) of God's kingdom (God's rule). He insisted that God is a loving Father. His favorite noun for God was not the common Jewish name for God, "Yahweh." According to our sources he never used the ineffable tetragrammaton. He customarily called God *Abba*, "Father." He also taught his disciples to call God by this unsophisticated term of endearment.

He possibly faced without fear the premonition that he would be murdered, perhaps stoned. After an unknown period of public teaching in Galilee he moved southward to Jerusalem, where he boldly and successfully demonstrated his disdain for the corruption in the Temple cult. The so-called episode in which he knocked over the tables of the money changers reveals that he publicly confronted the priestly establishment. He suffered through rejection by two close disciples, the betrayal of Judas and the denial of Peter. He eventually died ignominiously on a cross, outside the western wall of Jerusalem in the spring of 30 C.E. Within a very short interval of time his followers, despite their initial doubts, began to claim boldly and openly that God had raised him from the dead.

THE SELF-UNDERSTANDING OF THE HISTORICAL JESUS

What did Jesus think about his inability to convince his closest disciples that he must face a life of suffering and that the rule of God was beginning to break into the present? What did he think about his constant rejection, first by scribes and Pharisees and then finally by his closest disciples, including Judas and Peter? What was he trying to do in the Temple when he attacked the money changers? What was his relation to or role in the rule of God? Did the healing miracles hinder his search for self-understanding? While it is certain that he was not absorbed in a search for self-understanding, did he ponder who he was and his role in God's drama of salvation? Why had he been baptized by John the Baptist? Who did he think he was, and what enabled him to speak so confidently and authoritatively? Did he fear martyrdom, or did he expect it? Are there any of his sayings that reflect not so much the confessions of his followers as his own personal self-understanding?

Answers to some of these intriguing questions are hidden in one of his parables. These well-known art forms are characteristically typical of Jesus' means of teaching. The Parable of the Wicked Tenant Farmers probably derives ultimately from Jesus. First, it is widely attested and cannot be attributed to the creativity of one evangelist. It is found within and outside the Christian canon. Second, the essential core of this parable is different from the proclamations (*kerygmata*) of Jesus' earliest followers. The concept of the "son" is thoroughly Jewish and contains none of the distinctive early christological reflections. The death of the "son" is not by crucifixion; the corpse is dishonored, and the death is in no way efficacious. Third, the parable bears the stamp of Jesus' own genius; it was not transferred to him from an unknown Jewish source. It is an eschatological parable and thus coheres exactly with other well-known parables of Jesus. Fourth, the setting of the parable, especially the social and economic life portrayed, reflects Jesus' own time and not that of the evangelists. The fruitful farms are owned by absentee landlords, as was the case beginning with Herod the Great but not after the horrifying destruction and conquest of Palestine by the Romans in 70 C.E. Fifth, the reference to the "son" is impressively undeveloped and ambiguous; and this factor accords well with the use of "son" in early Jewish theology, and especially in the words of some Galilean charismatics contemporaneous with Jesus. Sixth, the parable is sewn with one piece of cloth; it does not evidence patching and reworking by the redactional activity of the evangelists.

It is wise now to highlight the Parable of the Wicked Tenant Farmers, which is recorded in Mark 12:1–12, Matthew 21:33–46, Luke 20:9–19, and also in the Gospel of Thomas 65. Previous studies, confirmed by my own research, have disclosed that the two primary records of this parable are in Mark, which was one (perhaps *the*) source for Matthew and Luke, and in the Gospel of Thomas, which preserves also an early and independent version. Here is my translation of Mark's tradition:

> And he began to speak to them in parables. "A man planted a vineyard, and set a fence around it, and dug a trough (for the wine press), and built a tower, and leased it to tenants; then he went away. When the time came (for the harvest), he sent a servant to the tenants, to collect from them (his portion) of the

fruits of the vineyard. But they took him, beat (him), and sent (him) away empty-handed. Again he sent to them another servant, him they wounded in the head, and treated shamefully. And he sent another, him they killed; then many others, some they beat but some they killed. He had still one other: a beloved son [*huion agapeton*]. He sent him to them last [of all, *eschaton*] saying, 'They will respect my son.' But those tenants said to one another, 'This is the heir; come, let us kill him, and the inheritance will be ours.' And seizing (him), they killed him, and cast him out of the vineyard. What will the owner [*ho kyrios*] of the vineyard do? He will come and destroy the tenants, and give the vineyard to others." (Mark 12:1–9)

Critical research (especially Form Criticism) shows that this story has a definite beginning and ending; it is a short, self-contained pericope and story.

There is impressive evidence that this parable once circulated in Aramaic, or at least in a Semitic language. Note the undeveloped sentences and the need to supply full meaning by the use of parentheses. This phenomenon is atypical of Koine Greek, but is customary with Semitic languages. Note especially the need to supply objective pronouns: recall "But they took him, beat (him), and sent (him) away empty-handed." Like English, Greek usually represents these objective pronouns. In Aramaic, the language of Jesus and his earliest followers, these are often assumed.

The story is not invented by the Evangelist Mark. He did, of course, edit (redact) it. He contributed the beginning and transition for his own Gospel: "And he began to speak to them in parables." He supplied "beloved" before son. The title "beloved son" is clearly a Marcan redaction, as we know from studying his account of Jesus' baptism and transfiguration. In the Marcan record we are presented with the theophonic voice: "You (or this is) my beloved son" (Mark 1:11, 9:7). No other Marcan addition is obvious. It is certain that Mark did not create this story or parable. It is also unlikely that one of Jesus' early followers composed the parable. The use of the noun "son" is not developed and remains frustratingly ambiguous. The death of the "son" — surely meant to be Jesus in the synoptic tradition — does not parallel what is known about the death of Jesus. He died on a cross outside the walls of Jerusalem. The "son" in the parable dies by some unknown means *within* the vineyard. According to the earliest records, Jesus' corpse was revered and treated with respect. In the parable the corpse of the son is cast with contempt over the wall of the vineyard.

It is highly probable, therefore, that this parable derives ultimately from Jesus. Before attempting to discern whether Jesus' own self-understanding can be determined from this parable, we must confront the possibility that Mark added not only "beloved" but also "son." This initial possibility becomes highly unlikely when we recognize (*pace* N. Perrin and others) that this term was not invented in the early Christian communities. It is found also in early Jewish literature and was associated with Galilean miracle workers.[21]

Most importantly, "son" cannot be attributed to Marcan redaction; it is also found in the Gospel of Thomas, which is independent of Mark. Note the parable according to this extra-canonical gospel:[22]

> He (Jesus) said: A good man had a vineyard. He leased it to tenant (farmers) so that they might cultivate it, and he might collect (his share of) its fruit from them. He sent his servant so that the tenants might give him (some of) the fruit of the vineyard. They, however, seized his servant. They beat him; a little longer and they would have killed him. The servant departed; (and) told it to his master. His master said: "Perhaps he did not know them"[23] He sent another servant; the tenants beat him as well. Then the master sent his son. He said: "Perhaps they will respect my son."[24] Since those tenants knew that he was the heir of the vineyard, they seized him; they killed him.[25] He who has ears let him hear.

We have now seen that "son" is found both in the Greek of Mark and in the Coptic Gospel of Thomas. These two Gospels are not dependent on each other; scholarly research has established that this parable in the Gospel of Thomas is not derived from the Gospel of Mark. The Gospel of Mark, which dates from around 70 C.E., cannot have borrowed from the Gospel of Thomas, which reached its present form around 125 C.E.

In both versions the parable is quasi-allegorical. The owner of the vineyard is surely God. The vineyard is the well-known symbol for Israel and Jerusalem. Earlier we saw that the Righteous Teacher inherited the biblical concept of God's "planting the eternal planting."[26] Here in this parable we see the image

of the vineyard; God has planted and cultivated Israel. Recall
again the famous allegory of the vineyard, Israel:

> Let me sing for my beloved
>   my love song concerning his vineyard...
> For the vineyard of the LORD of hosts
>   is the house of Israel,
> and the people of Judah
>   are his pleasant planting;...
>
> (Isa. 5:1–7; NRSV)

Jesus apparently originated the allegorical Parable of the
Wicked Tenant Farmers. He referred to God as the owner and
cultivator of the vineyard, Israel. He stressed the history of salvation, the rejection of the prophets, and the failures of those
sent to Israel to call her back from sin and to the obedience of
faithfulness to the covenant with God.

Most importantly he included himself in the review of the
history of salvation. He emphasized that last of all God sent
his "son." What did Jesus intend by this dimension of the allegory? What did he think of himself? Do the words reflect
self-understanding?

Convincing answers to these questions will obviously be
less impressive than the questions themselves. As we continue in the attempt to discern something of Jesus' self-
understanding, let us keep in mind the insights already obtained from the brief examination of the allegory composed by
the Righteous Teacher.

The setting of the psalm by the founder of the Qumran
Community is very different from the social setting of the parable. The Righteous Teacher saw himself as living in the desert,
far removed from the Temple. For him "the Land" was in need
of redemption, because of the illegitimate false priests and the
corrupted cult. Jesus, however, living in the same "Holy Land"
knew the pain of occupation by the Romans. The land promised to Abraham and his descendants, including the Righteous
Teacher and Jesus, was occupied. The Jews were forced to lease
from foreigners farms once belonging to them and their fathers.
Well-known terms — like land and fruit — took on religious
and, at times, revolutionary significance.

JESUS AND THE RIGHTEOUS TEACHER

Like the Righteous Teacher, Jesus saw himself playing a major part in the economy of God's salvation of his world and people. The Righteous Teacher had a very strong ego; he began his psalm with the use of the first person pronoun singular. He is convinced who he is. The whole psalm reflects his celebration of his own special role. He is attempting to defend his own exilic condition. Jesus never uses the first personal pronoun singular. His parable does climax with the sending of the son; but the latter noun is used in an oblique manner. Its precise meaning is never given. Both the Righteous Teacher and Jesus are convinced of their unique place in God's schema for history and time. The Righteous Teacher struggles to defend his own status and role and his exiled condition; Jesus, however, intimates his own martyrdom as he walks steadfastly toward Jerusalem.

Both men are partly characteristic of the sociological categories of charismatic and prophet. Both perceived that they were living at the end of all normal time and history. For each of them the drama of salvation was almost at its end. There is certainly some difference, however, between the Righteous Teacher's looking forward to the growth of the "shoot," which is still in the future, but in the not too distant future, and Jesus' reference to the sending of the son. For Jesus the coming of the "son" is not futuristic; he is the son. In this sense Jesus' concept of the End of Time is more present-oriented than that of the Righteous Teacher. The contrast here must not be exaggerated; the shoot is present — to a certain extent — in the planting, the garden.

The Righteous Teacher's group was destroyed by the Romans in 68 C.E. Jesus was crucified by the Romans in 30; but his group continued, and eventually — obviously in a modified form — established the religion of the Roman Empire.

Each of these two pre-70 Palestinian Jews professed a very different source for his own self-understanding. The Righteous Teacher perceived the meaning of his own life because of the presence of his own little band of priests who were faithful to him, and to him alone. For him, "the trees of life" were chosen by God to obey him, to listen to the mystery revealed only to him. Through them God was establishing the eternal paradisiacal garden.

Jesus never obtained such support from his little band of Jews. The disciples failed to comprehend his message and did not follow him to the end. He died alone and deserted. According to Mark and Thomas, Jesus' only source for self-understanding was God, his Father. Mark has the Lord of the vineyard — that is, God — say about the final messenger: "They will respect my son." The possessive pronoun is powerfully symbolic. The son belongs to God. We are left without further guidance in attempting to discern what Jesus may have meant when he reflexively included himself in the drama of salvation as the son.

Surely he would not have agreed with the early Greek church fathers. They claimed that Jesus was of the same and identical substance as God. Jesus did not use such categories. We are much closer to his probable self-understanding when we reflect on the meaning of Psalm 2:

> I will tell of the decree of the LORD:
> He said to me, "You are my son,
> today I have begotten you."
>   (Ps. 2:7; NRSV)

CONCLUSION

A perceptive reading of a psalm in a Dead Sea Scroll discloses the self-understanding of the Righteous Teacher, the founder of the Qumran Community. A critical analysis of the Parable of the Wicked Tenant Farmers reveals the self-understanding of Jesus of Nazareth. Both men reveal how they saw themselves engaged in God's work and within the age-old prophetic movement.

One gifted Jew, a Jerusalem priest, withdrew from the Temple cult and lived in the desert. The other charismatic Jew went from his home in Galilee and boldly entered Jerusalem, the seat of the opposition against him. One story ended in 68 C.E. in the flames of the monastery where the Righteous Teacher had lived. The other story continues today.

One Jew remains anonymous; the other became eponymous. Some of the reasons may reside in their different, yet so similar, self-understandings.

NOTES

1. G. Jeremias, *Der Lehrer der Gerechtigkeit*, Studien zur Umwelt des Neuen Testaments 2 (Göttingen, 1963), esp. see 249–64.

2. For critical, philological, and bibliographical notes see my "An Allegorical and Autobiographical Poem by the Moreh Has-Sedek (1QH 8:4–11)," in *Sha'arei Talmon*, ed. Weston W. Fields (Winona Lake, Ill.: Eisenbrauns, 1992), 295–307.

3. The author, the Righteous Teacher, is meditating upon his exile in the desert of Judaea. There is no spring or fountain at or near Qumran. The use of water, especially "living water," is highly metaphorical and symbolic of salvific water. This meaning of "living water" is not found in biblical Hebrew; in the Old Testament this term refers to running water.

4. The Righteous Teacher is the (source of) water for "the trees of life," who are his followers.

5. Literally, "the waterer of" the garden (Hiphil participle construct singular), or "cup bearer" (noun construct singular). The noun obtains the meaning "irrigation" in post-second-century Jewish Rabbinic writings.

6. Asterisks denote the place where a new line begins in the scroll.

7. The images of the Garden of Eden and of Paradise seem to be behind the thought here.

8. Either the author later develops the concept of the *Yaḥad* (oneness), "the Community," from such seminal reflections and experiences, or he is alluding to this meaning here.

9. Literally, "those who hide themselves" (Pual).

10. Note the clear evidence of Qumranic dualism. Here the terms are "the trees of life," who are to be identified with "the Sons of Light," and "the trees of the water," who are not only "the Sons of Darkness," but indeed the wicked priests officiating in the Temple cult.

The imagery causes some confusion, since "the trees of life" have access to the water source, and "water" has a very positive salvific meaning in the Qumran Scrolls. Well known to our author is Psalm 1:3, which lauds the righteous who are like "a tree planted by streams of water."

It is probable that Ezekiel 31 and the Allegory of the Cedar shaped the symbolic allegory of the Righteous Teacher. Note especially Ezekiel 31:14:

> All this is in order that no trees by the waters may grow to lofty height or set their tops among the clouds, and that no trees that drink water may reach up to them in height.

> For all of them are handed over to death,
> to the world below;
> along with all mortals,
> with those who go down to the Pit. (NRSV)

Here, in order, we have significant biblical symbolisms for our psalm's "trees of the water," the symbolism of height, and the death of the water trees.

11. The "mysterious water source" is the Righteous Teacher. This identification is clarified by line 11, in which he refers to "his mystery" not being perceived.

12. As is well known this term *nṣr* is a highly symbolical term that refers to the coming shoot of David who will fulfill the promises of God on this earth. This traditional meaning, however, must not be transported into these verses without careful examination of the precise context of this column.

13. The technical term *drk*, as we stated earlier about *yḥd*, is probably in an early stage of development. It is probable that after the time of the Righteous Teacher this phrase was understood to mean the following: "all transgressors of the Way."

14. The meaning seems to be that the branches shall be destroyed or impaired by the birds.

15. The allegory refers to the wicked priests in Jerusalem who have magnified themselves; one of them is serving as the high priest. The author is convinced that he and his followers are the only legitimate descendants of David's priests.

16. The implication is that like "the Sons of Darkness," according to 1QS 4, the evil trees (the "trees of the water") have no hope.

17. This person is to be identified with the Righteous Teacher. See line 4, in which he sees himself as the "irrigator" of the garden, and note the use of the Hiphil in both verbal forms.

18. This passage refers to the Righteous Teacher, who was the legitimate heir to the high priesthood in the Jerusalem Temple, but was not honored. He was banished from the Temple, along with his followers, because the mystery revealed to him by God (see 1QpHab 7) was unperceived, except by those loyal to him. The "trees of the water" are the "wicked" priests in Jerusalem; the "trees of life" are his followers who are living, because they have the source of life. Many of these thoughts are important background and foreground for the theology developed by the author and redactors of the Gospel of John.

19. See my *Jesus within Judaism*, Anchor Bible Reference Library 1 (New York: Doubleday, 1988).

20. This once hotly disputed issue is now solidly affirmed by M. Hengel, E. P. Sanders, and others. Their works are well known

and can be easily found in the bibliographical synopsis in *Jesus within Judaism*.

21. See my *Jesus within Judaism* and contributions on Honi and Hanina ben Dosa in the *Anchor Bible Dictionary*, ed. David Noel Freedman (New York: Doubleday, 1992).

22. The translation given is idiomatic.

23. The Coptic is amazing here. Any possible errors at this stage of the story are not attributed to the wicked tenant farmers. This linguistic device, I am persuaded, may well be an example of Jesus' use of rhetoric and irony.

24. Again, the attentive listener would be surprised. What kind of a father would be so reckless with the life of his own son? This intent seems authentic; it does fit with Jesus' concept of mission, with his willingness to suffer, and also with the Jewish (even earlier) traditions, especially those related to the prophets (see the pseudepigraphic book on the Lives and Deaths of the Prophets).

25. It is now abundantly clear. The tenants knew exactly what they were doing. They knew that the son was the heir. They intended to kill him.

26. Semites like to stress a point by repeating the main root idea; hence, we often hear about God who plants the eternal plant.

Chapter 3

Jesus and Judaism
in the New Testament

Leander Keck

The topic "Jesus and Judaism" turns out to be far more complex than we expect. For one thing, getting a fair and accurate picture of Judaism as Jesus knew it has proven to be difficult, partly because historians now have considerably more data with which to work and partly because the growing sophistication in the use of the data has made untenable the simpler generalizations of previous generations. Moreover, the historical task of recovering an unbiased picture of Jesus from the Gospels has also grown more difficult because in recent years scholars have become more alert to the complex and subtle factors that influenced the ways in which the New Testament writers deal with Jesus' relation to Judaism.

Four preliminary remarks about the title of this essay will expose important dimensions of the subject matter. Then I will look briefly at three New Testament writers. Some general observations will conclude the discussion.

PRELIMINARY REMARKS

The first preliminary remark has to do with the word "Judaism." The word *Ioudaismos* was coined by Greek-speaking Jews to identify the Jewish religion and culture as a whole, as a discrete and distinctive phenomenon in the Greco-Roman world. In 2 and 4 Maccabees, it is used to speak of a religious culture as a whole, as if from the point of view of the outsider. This usage is also found in the letters of Bishop Ignatius, who, writing around 115 of our era, uses it as the opposite of *Christianismos*. In the New Testament only Paul uses it, and only in Galatians (1:13–14), to speak of his pre-Christian life.[1] Never does the New Testament use the word "Judaism" in relation to Jesus. "Jesus and Judaism" is our own modern formulation. We use it, nonetheless, because it is a customary and convenient way of identifying a field of inquiry within which one can differentiate various kinds of "Judaisms" in the New Testament era.

Next and second, it is important to distinguish what is entailed in "Jesus and Judaism in the New Testament" from what is involved in "Jesus in Judaism." Because almost everything we can learn about Jesus is derived from the New Testament, it is easy to assume that the two topics are virtually interchangeable. In fact, it is just this assumption that has caused considerable mischief. So it is essential to see, albeit briefly, why the difference between the two topics should not be blurred, even if they overlap.

What comes into focus here is the difference between historical exegesis and historical reconstruction. "Jesus and Judaism in the New Testament" attempts to explain, understand, and interpret the relation of Jesus to Judaism as it appears in the New Testament texts. It is a historical enterprise insofar as one attempts to account for what these texts say (or imply) about the subject matter by placing *them* in their respective historical context. Whether their treatments of the subject matter are consistent with each other, complete, or correct (consonant with all the evidence) is another matter. In contrast, "Jesus in Judaism" attempts to explain, understand, and interpret the figure of Jesus by placing *him* as accurately as possible within the historical phenomenon of "Judaism." To do so, one must reconstruct both "Jesus" and "Judaism" by assembling as much reliable data, usually derived from a variety of sources, as possible.

To simplify: the former, "Jesus and Judaism in the New Testament," asks, "What does the New Testament say happened?,"
the latter, "Jesus in Judaism," asks, "What really happened?";
or "What, if any, is the difference between the report and the
event (to the extent that we can reconstruct it)?" In principle, all
sources (texts, inscriptions, coins, archaeological evidence, etc.)
should be interpreted before one derives historically reliable evidence from them; their purposes, limitations, and biases need
to be taken into account lest one simply repeat what they say.

Third, having distinguished the two topics, it is essential
to note briefly that the relation between them has a particular history, one that we inherit. Ever since the beginnings
of modern critical historiography in the Enlightenment, historians have been "professional skeptics" — they have refused
to accept as "fact" any report until it has been tested. Consequently, historians pursuing the theme of "Jesus and Judaism"
doubted, as a matter of principle, that what the New Testament said was historically accurate until it could be shown to
be probably true. Inevitably, considerable doubt arose whether
the New Testament portrait was historically correct. Moreover,
one motive driving the historical study of Jesus has been the
conviction that the truth of Christianity would have a firmer
foundation if it rested on solid facts rather than on reports from
the texts. This suggested, at least to some, that "the real Jesus"[2]
was to be found *in* Judaism rather than in Christianity, which
allegedly made a god out of a Jew.[3] In other words, the older
liberal Protestant critical study of Jesus drove a wedge between
the Christian interpretation of Jesus in the New Testament and
Jesus himself; the "historical Jesus" was the Jesus in Judaism.

Those who promoted the "historical Jesus" as the surer
foundation for Christian faith in him did not suspect the di-
lemma they were creating. The more Jesus was painted into the
Jewish landscape the less he stood out, and the less he stood
out the less reason there was to single him out as the one
who was decisive. So the pressure was on to show historically
that at every point that mattered, Jesus transcended Judaism.
He could be in Judaism but not really of it. In other words, in
order to show historically that Jesus merits our faith, scholars
were driven to show that Jesus was superior to the Judaism that
surrounded him. To do so, they often created an unhistorical
picture of Judaism as a religion of either harsh and barren le-

galism or of overheated apocalyptic illusions.[4] The reason for this is not simply that Christian scholars were incorrigibly anti-Semitic. The real reason lies in the idea that a more sound Christian religion could be based on facts that were established historically. Once one decides to base faith on facts, then one's allegiance to Jesus must be based on facts about Jesus, and the only way to justify loyalty to Jesus instead of Hillel or some other teacher is to show that Jesus is better, more profound, more spiritual, less parochial, and free of apocalyptic notions about the end of the world.

Fortunately, the prejudicial portrayal of Judaism is no longer credible in contemporary scholarship, though one can still find it. Fortunate also is the discovery that history cannot establish the superiority of Jesus. And this means that allegiance to Jesus cannot be based on the results of history, because the Jesus of history is ambiguous.[5] This means that whoever follows Jesus does so because this Jewish figure is interpreted in a particular way. Without this interpretive framework, Jesus in Judaism is just another interesting first-century Palestinian teacher from whom we may learn. In other words, the decisiveness of Jesus for faith becomes visible and plausible only within an interpretive framework that includes and transcends history without cancelling it.

This brings us to the fourth preliminary remark. The most important frameworks for understanding Jesus' relation to Judaism are those in the New Testament. They are not the only ones. There is a Muslim framework that regards Jesus as a prophet, just as there is a Hindu framework that sees him as one of a series of avatars or manifestations of an eternal principle. While it would be useful to compare these interpretive frameworks, I will not do so. My aim is to help us understand and appreciate three interpretive frameworks in the New Testament. They will invite us to think afresh about Jesus and Judaism.

MATTHEW

The Gospel According to Matthew has the reputation of being the most Jewish Gospel in the New Testament while at the same time being an anti-Jewish Gospel like John. I continue to think that Matthew was written around about 90 C.E. in the general

area around Antioch, where there was a large Jewish community. Twenty years before, Judaism underwent its great shock
when the Romans captured Jerusalem. As a result, the Temple
was burned and the priestly Sadducees disappeared from the
scene, as did the Essenes at Qumran who first hid their scrolls
in the desert caves. The one group that survived was the Pharisees, who were now consolidating their influence and laying
the foundations for the Rabbinic Judaism that followed. Consequently, Matthew's readers confronted a Judaism that was
closing its ranks, forcing Jewish Christians to choose between
their Jewish heritage and Christian identity. What Jesus pre-
dicts in Matthew 10 actually refers to Matthew's own time:
Christians will be flogged in the synagogue, brothers will betray brothers, parents betray children, and children the parents
(10:18–21). Matthew no longer expects that the Jewish people
will believe that Jesus is the Messiah.

The Gospel of Matthew used traditions about Jesus, who
lived forty years before the fall of Jerusalem, but shaped them
into an account about Jesus for use in a church that faced a new
form of Judaism as a result of that disaster.[6] This means that
Matthew used material about Jesus in Judaism in order to write
a gospel about Jesus and Judaism. As a result, the Matthean
Jesus stands over against Judaism more or less as the Matthean
readers do. Matthew's readers know a hostile synagogue but
may have never seen a Sadducee; and the Pharisees they know
differed from those mentioned in the stories about Jesus. Three
questions will bring into focus the effect of Matthew's situation
on the way it portrays Jesus and Judaism.

1. *How does Matthew portray the Judaism to which Jesus is related?* To begin with, one would never detect from Matthew that
in Jesus' day Judaism had many faces, or, as we would say, was
pluralistic. If we had only Matthew we would not surmise that
there were Essenes either in the Palestinian villages or west of
the Dead Sea. Nor would we guess that much of Palestinian
Jewry was deeply Hellenized. Matthew is simply not interested in presenting Jesus in a historically accurate and balanced
picture of Judaism. Moreover, apart from Jesus' parents, Jesus
himself, and his disciples, Matthew gives us only three names
of individual Jews: John the Baptist, Joseph of Arimathea, and
Caiaphas the High Priest. With but one exception (8:19) Jewish
leaders appear in groups of unspecified size: scribes, Pharisees,

Sadducees, priests, and chief priests. Matthew does not explain who they are or what distinguishes one group from another. Either Matthew assumes that the readers know enough about Palestine sixty years before to need no information, or it regards the differences as relatively unimportant because all these groups represent the religious establishment. The latter is the more likely. In other words, the Evangelist Matthew is not ignorant of the differences within the Judaism of Jesus' day but generally indifferent to them because his eye is on the conflict between Jesus and the leaders of Judaism, a conflict that intensifies as the story develops.[7]

Further, Matthew shows Jesus in relation to three institutions of Judaism: the synagogue, the Temple, and the Sanhedrin. Several times we read that Jesus preached in the synagogues (9:35; 13:54), but we learn nothing about the synagogue itself or what Jesus said there. What we do learn is that healing a withered hand in the synagogue on the Sabbath triggered a plot against Jesus (12:9–14). About the Temple too Matthew tells us nothing. It is, however, the place where Jesus' confrontation with the Jewish leaders reaches its climax. In Matthew, Jesus not only expelled those who sold what was needed to maintain the sacrificial system, but healed people and on the following day silenced the opposition (21:12–22:46). Having made his point Jesus left the Temple and pronounced its impending destruction (24:1–2). The Sanhedrin appears only in connection with the trial of Jesus (26:59), though it is twice mentioned in a saying of Jesus (5:22; 10:17).

Fourth, of the Jewish festivals, the only one that is mentioned is the Passover, because this figures prominently in the Passion story. About New Year, Day of Atonement, Pentecost, Succoth, we hear nothing at all. Sabbath is mentioned because it is the necessary setting for the conflict over its observance, but about its role in Judaism Matthew is silent.

To sum up, what Matthew says about Judaism is virtually nothing. Of its multifaceted character he mentions only those elements that are necessary for the story of Jesus' conflicts with the religious leaders — a conflict that does not end even with Jesus' death (28:11–15). Matthew is more sympathetic to the Jewish people; for he not only portrays the crowds as responding to Jesus (9:35–38; 15:29–31), but reports that he had compassion for them. Still, before the story is over, the leadership corrupts the crowds, so that they join in the demand for Jesus' death. At the climax of this opposition, Matthew reports they shouted, "Let him be crucified!" (27:23) and that when Pilate pronounced him innocent, "all the people answered, 'His blood be on us and on our children'" (27:25). In other words, in Matthew, Jesus is ever more alienated from Judaism.

2. *Is Matthew interested only in Jesus versus Judaism? Is there only opposition?* That would be too simple, too stark, and without enough subtlety. This judgment rests on two considerations. First is the fact that Matthew emphasizes more than any other New Testament book that Jesus fulfills Scripture and Israel's hope. From the "begats" onward, Matthew reminds the reader of this theme. Seven times Matthew actually points out that what we have just read happened as the fulfillment of Scripture (1:22; 2:15, 23; 4:14–16; 8:17; 12:17–21; 13:35; 21:4). But this Evangelist also shows that Jesus is like Moses, first as a baby who was nearly killed by a king (2:13–18) and then by bringing God's Law on a mountain (chaps. 5–7). Moreover, Matthew's Jesus explicitly limits the mission of the disciples to the lost sheep of the house of Israel and tells them to avoid the gentiles, of whom there were many in the Galilee of the day (10:5). And when Jesus rides into Jerusalem on an ass's colt, he comes as the king spoken of by the prophet Zechariah, and over his thorn-crowned head on the cross is nailed the charge: "King of the Jews." Indeed, the language of the Passion story echoes again and again the words of the Old Testament, for Matthew has told the story of Jesus as the one in whom the words of Scripture become event.

That "Jesus versus Judaism" is too simple is clear also from a second consideration: Matthew's Jesus says unambiguously what God's will is. And this will is nothing other than what the Scripture of Judaism has also said. This is especially clear in chapter 15, in which the Pharisees and scribes come from Jerusalem, the center of Judaism, to ask why the disciples transgress the traditions of the elders and do not wash their hands when they eat. This is not a matter of eating with dirty hands but with hands that have not been ritually cleansed. (The Pharisees' were taking the rules that applied to the priests in the Temple and applying them to themselves, laymen, and to all the people, so that the whole nation would be a kingdom of priests, a holy people, just as the Bible said; Exod. 19:6.) Instead of answering the question put to him, Jesus takes the initiative and attacks the Pharisees for emphasizing the traditions of the elders, the oral Torah. The Pharisees believed that the unwritten Torah, the oral tradition, was as much a part of God's revelation at Sinai as what was written. But not Jesus. He accuses them of annulling God's word in order to hold on to the traditions (15:6).

In chapter 23, Matthew has Jesus affirm that the scribes and Pharisees sit on Moses' seat — that is, they interpret the Law of Moses. So do what they say but do not do as they do (23:1–3). In the following sevenfold denunciation of the scribes and Pharisees as "hypocrites," Jesus accuses them of missing the point of the Scriptures that they do know. Again and again he makes it clear that he does not bring a new Law of God, but states the meaning of the Law they already had but obscured by tradition and self-serving interpretation. It is Matthew's Jesus who says that he did not come to destroy the Law and the prophets but to fulfill them (5:17–20). In a word, in Matthew Jesus opposes Judaism in the name of God's will in its own Scripture. In so doing, he does not want to displace Judaism but to bring it back to its real center.[8]

3. *What, then, is Jesus' relation to Judaism in Matthew?* Simply this: because Jesus is the one in whom Scripture is fulfilled, the King of Israel, the Wisdom of God and the Son of God, Judaism's rejection of Jesus is the rejection of its own fulfillment and future. As the conclusion to the parable says, the kingdom will be taken away from them and given to others (21:44). In other words, from Matthew's angle the relation of Jesus to Judaism is tragic. Because Jesus *in* Judaism was rejected, he became the doom of the Judaism that rejected him.

This perspective, combined with the fact that early Christians used those traditions about Jesus that helped them in their own conflicts with Judaism, explains why Matthew emphasizes the points of tension between Jesus and the Judaism of his day. All points of continuity are bypassed, leaving us to guess (probably rightly) that he observed Sabbath and festivals, as well as food laws. One can hardly expect a community that is defining itself over against another group to have emphasized the continuity between its founder and the current opposition. Even so, in Matthew the theme of Jesus and Judaism is played out within Judaism. Matthew's Jesus stands over against Judaism just like the Old Testament prophets stood over against the religion of Israel.

JOHN

The Gospel According to John, interestingly enough, comes not only from the same time (about 90–95 C.E.) but, I believe, also from the same place — Antioch or its vicinity. Both Gospels reflect the growing tension between the church and the synagogue. What is distinctive about John, however, is that the narrator speaks of Jesus' opponents as "the Jews" — as if Jesus himself were not a Jew. And Jesus distances himself from Judaism when he refers to the Torah as "your law" (John 8:17; 10:34). Recent study of John, as of Matthew, has explored the history and situation of the community in which this Gospel was formed and thereby has come to emphasize its Jewish character and context. It appears that the Christian Jews had experienced increased hostility from the synagogue that at first tolerated them and had recently been excluded from it (reflected in the anachronistic statement in 9:22, and in Jesus' prediction in 16:2). Jesus' disputes with "the Jews" therefore reflect this later alienation.[9] At the same time, John retains its Jewish character because many of its traditions are traceable to their Palestinian origins. Some of these traditions contain accurate local information (e.g., the pool in Jerusalem, 5:2–3); others use language that is thoroughly Jewish, such as the epithet "Samaritan" hurled at Jesus in 8:48 or "sons of light" in 12:36, which is common in the Dead Sea Scrolls.[10]

Again, we begin by asking how Judaism is portrayed here. Generally speaking, we learn more about Judaism in John than in Matthew. Also in John we meet Pharisees (one of whom is named Nicodemus) and priests, but we do not hear of Sadducees any more than we do of Essenes. But we encounter Samaritans and learn both that they do not regard Jerusalem as the legitimate place of worship and that Jews have no dealings with Samaritans (4:21, 9). As in Matthew, we hear also about synagogue and Temple. Although Jesus tells the High Priest, "I have always taught in synagogues and in the Temple" (18:20), only once does John place Jesus' teaching in the synagogue (almost as an afterthought, 6:59), but he has Jesus teach in the Temple several times (7:28–31; 8:20; 10:22–30). What distinguishes John, however, is the fact that he organizes the story around Jewish festivals: three Passovers (2:19–22; 6:4; 12:55), Tabernacles (7:1), Hanukkah (10:22), and an unnamed "feast" (5:1). But again, New Year, Day of Atonement, and Pentecost are missing. We learn also some details about Jewish customs — the water jars at Cana are for ritual purification (2:6), the Passover-Sabbath is a special Sabbath (19:31); Jews were concerned about not being ritually impure for Passover (18:28). We learn that one may circumcise on the Sabbath (7:22) because the oral Torah allows it. Such details, coupled with the many place names, give John's reader a more vivid picture of the setting of Jesus' word and deed than Matthew provides.

In John, Jesus never uses the word "hypocrite" to denounce the Pharisees. They are portrayed as having great influence, so much that even the unnamed authorities who believed in Jesus would not admit it "for fear of the Pharisees...lest they should be put out of the synagogue" (12:42). Throughout, the Pharisees and chief priests together plot against Jesus (7:32; 11:47, 57; 18:3), but it is the Pharisees who oppose him most resolutely. Indeed, they speak for the Jewish religion and the Jews. In fact, a basic feature of this Gospel is that Jews, Judaism, Pharisees, and priests all flow into one another, with little differentiation.

The Johannine Jesus stands over against this relatively undifferentiated entity of Judaism and Jews, and the conclusion of the Prologue states the reason: "the Law was given through Moses; grace and truth came through Jesus Christ" — as if there were no grace or truth in the Law (1:17). Yet Moses is said to have written about Christ (1:45). So the Jews are indicted for not really believing Moses, even if they claim to be his disciples (9:28); if they had, they would have believed Jesus too (5:45–46). It is not simply that under Pharisaic influence they distorted the Law. The resistance to the claims of Jesus and to his word shows that no one keeps the Law (7:19).

So in John the issue between Jesus and Judaism is not the right way to obey Moses and achieve righteousness, as in Matthew. In fact, righteousness in this sense is not part of the Johannine vocabulary. The issue between them is Jesus himself. In a word, in John the Jews and Judaism represent the unbelieving world as it refuses to acknowledge Jesus as the Creator, the Logos incarnate, who is the interpreter of God (1:18). Therefore, what in Matthew appears at the end — the self-condemnation of the Jews in calling for Jesus' death — is the thread that runs through the whole story in John. One cannot reject the incarnate Logos without incurring self-condemnation. This is why John shows the Pharisees and the Jews as repeatedly either misunderstanding what Jesus says or flatly rejecting it.

Now, by any ordinary criteria the Jews are right. When Jesus claims to be the bread from heaven, they say that they know very well where he comes from because they know his parents (6:41–42). When he says that whoever eats this bread will live forever, why should not the Jews ask, "How can this man give us his flesh to eat?" (6:52)? When he says that they cannot go where he is going, why should they not wonder whether he is planning a trip to the diaspora (7:32–35) or even whether he is planning suicide (8:21–22)? In other words, the Jews misunderstand because they take Jesus' words at face value, while he uses them in a different sense, a sense that John's Christian readers understand. By this literary device — double meaning — the Gospel of John underlines the disparity between the perspective of Jesus and the world.

Moreover, in John Jesus is often the aggressor, attacking the Jews — the sharpest charge being that they are of the devil (8:44). We can sympathize not only with the Jews of John but also with the Jews of today, who are offended by such a Jesus. Yet it must be said that because the Jews represent the unbelieving world, the Johannine Jesus would have said the same things about Greeks if the incarnation had occurred in Greece. If someone today were to claim for himself what John's Jesus claims, we would scarcely be less offended. We might not crucify him, but we might have him put into an institution.

The force of these observations is clear. The Gospel is written in such a way that the reader of John faces the same decision about Jesus as did the Jews. Is he who he claims to be, and does he give what he claims to give, eternal life? Getting more historical information about Jesus, his family life, his education, or the context in which he lived does not make answering that question easier. John does not want us to correct the portrait of Jesus with historical facts, or even less to pity the Jews for not seeing who Jesus really is, but rather wants us to see ourselves in them, so that we are as confronted by the incarnate Logos as they were.

PAUL

In moving from Matthew and John to Paul, we not only step forty years closer to Jesus but change from narrative to analysis and argument. We now look at an interpreter who was a contemporary of Jesus (though they seem never to have met) and who had been a zealous advocate of that form of Judaism that in Matthew and John produced Jesus' most persistent critics and foes, Pharisaism (Phil. 3:4–6). Moreover, we recall that one of the points at issue between them was Jesus' rejection of the oral traditions, the unwritten Law. And Paul himself writes to the Galatians that he had been so extremely zealous for these traditions that he had tried to destroy the church before it got rooted too deeply (Gal. 1:13–16). It is interesting to speculate what Paul the zealous Pharisee and Jesus would have said to one another had they met. Such speculation, however, I leave to novelists. Still, we expect that this ex-Pharisee would have a good deal to say about Jesus and Pharisaic Judaism. Of all the writers in the New Testament, he would know best where the shoe had pinched. In fact, however, he says not a word about our topic; at the same time, what he does say is important for it.

Paul wrote in the 50s, about a decade before the revolt against Rome that ended with the destruction of the Temple. He seems not to have anticipated this uprising, to which Matthew and John could look back. Therefore there was nothing on Paul's horizon that he could regard as God's punishment of the Jews for rejecting Jesus. What Paul wrestles with in Romans 9–11 is the Jews' rejection of the gospel, not of Jesus. There is only one passage in which it looks like Paul blames the Jews for Jesus' death and sees in their fate God's punishment, namely, 1 Thessalonians 2:14–16. But I am among those who regard this as a later addition to the text, a view not held by everyone. In any case, in Paul's day the lines between church and synagogue were not yet hard. Jews who believed that Jesus was the Messiah were still a sect within Judaism. The kind of expulsion from the synagogue that John and Matthew assume had not yet been experienced widely. Above all, Paul wrote for Christians in Anatolia, Greece, and Rome, and most of his readers were gentiles who, we may assume, had little knowledge of Judaism in Palestine. The Judaism they knew was that of the Hellenistic synagogue, which attracted gentiles who accepted Jewish monotheism and ethics, but not necessarily the Jewish rituals.

So it is understandable that whereas Matthew and John, who work with traditions about Jesus, give at least some glimpses into the Judaism that Jesus knew, Paul says not a word about it. Because the Evangelists write the story of Jesus' ministry, they must deal with his relation to Judaism because it is unavoidable; because Paul does not write a story but interprets the meaning of Jesus into new situations of his largely gentile churches, he does not need to deal with the topic directly — though at a certain point he might have.

If we gather up the scattered references to Jesus in the seven undoubtedly genuine letters,[11] we get something like this: Jesus was a descendant of David, born into Judaism ("under the Law," Gal. 4:4). He exercised his ministry as a "servant of the circumcision" (Rom. 15:8). Whether Paul knew that Judas betrayed Jesus depends on how one translates the Greek verb *paredothe* in 1 Corinthians 11:23, where Paul repeats the tradition of the Lord's Supper. The customary translation is "in the night when he was betrayed," but it can also be rendered as "in the night he was handed over" — that is, by God, to death. The same tradition has Jesus say that "this cup is the new covenant in my blood" — that is, in my death. A few chapters later, Paul repeats another tradition, which says that "Christ died for our sins in accordance with the scriptures" (1 Cor. 15:3)." Paul knew, of course, that Jesus was crucified, that his body was buried, and that on the third day he was raised from the dead, as the old tradition also says (1 Cor. 15:3–5). Of Jesus' teachings, he mentions only a few, one forbidding divorce (1 Cor. 7:10–11) and the other that those who preach the gospel should get their living from it (1 Cor. 9:14). (Some scholars find many more echoes of Jesus' teaching than these two.) But Paul's letters have no reference to Jesus' preaching the kingdom of God, not a single hint that he had ever been in conflict with the Pharisees or priests, not a single miracle story, not even one about healing on the Sabbath. Even when Paul discusses what a Christian may or may not eat (1 Cor. 8, 10; Rom. 14–15), he does not mention that Jesus too dealt with ritual impurity or the possibility of being defiled by not observing the rules for ritual purity. In a word, Paul never mentions the message of Jesus or the Judaism in which it functioned. How do we explain this?

We cannot retrace Paul's thinking; the steps by which he came to his conclusions are his secret. What we can do, however, is to grasp his thought in such a way that we can understand why he did not seem to be interested in Jesus' own tensions with Judaism.

For Paul, the pivot on which the Christian understanding turns is Jesus' cross and resurrection. In his view, resurrection is not resuscitation. The coming alive again of a corpse is not resurrection, because it must die again. Rather, for Paul resurrection is the radical transformation of one's psychosomatic existence. Closely associated with it was the idea that the resurrection was one of the things to happen at the End, with the arrival of the Age to Come, the radical alternative to all of history. Today many of us have trouble with the idea of resurrection as such, wondering whether such a thing is possible. Paul's question, however, was whether it had happened in one case only — that of the crucified Jesus. If it had, then the New Age had dawned. Moreover, the New Age was, by definition, that state of affairs in which sin and death are overcome.

Moreover, for Paul sin and death enslave the self. In Paul's view, the human predicament is not that we commit sins and transgressions, violate rules of behavior. Rather, because we are human beings we are subject to sin and death before we commit any sin or transgression. Consequently, Paul is not interested in talking about individual sins and forgiveness of sins. What interests him is redemption, emancipation from the malign fate of sin and death. This is a human predicament, not a Jewish or Greek one. It is clear to Paul that obedience to the Law of God cannot redeem the self from sin because the Law makes us aware of sin (Rom. 3:20). In fact, he implies that "law" is something to which we are also in bondage, be it the Law of Moses or a gentile moral law. For Paul, law is a structure of obligation. In the case of the Law of Moses, it was not an eternal law anyway, as the Pharisees taught, but something that God gave through Moses (Gal. 3:17) in order to deal with human sin, but in the last analysis it is not able to do so. Sin is more powerful than Law (Rom. 8:3). Nor can obeying the Law deal with death, even if the Law were obeyed perfectly. The only way to be liberated from this bondage is by participating in the one event in which God broke the power of sin and death — Jesus and his resurrection. Whoever believes that God resurrected Jesus and is baptized becomes a participant in Christ, and whoever does this is emancipated from the tyranny of sin and death even though one still commits sins and must die (Rom. 6:5–11). Paul can also put this in a different idiom and say that whoever entrusts his or her life to God on the basis of the gospel is rightly related to God (i.e., "justified"), or reconciled with God, thereby overcoming the hostility between creature and Creator (Rom. 5:1, 9–11).

This very abbreviated summary of Paul's thought about redemption is enough to show why Paul was not interested in Jesus' conflicts with the Pharisees over the right way to obey the Law. For Paul, we are not redeemed from sin and death by following Jesus, by heeding his teachings, nor are we freed from the tyranny of Law as a way of life by imitating Jesus' own relation to the Law. The only thing that frees us is trusting the gospel that God raised Jesus from the dead and participating in him by baptism. This is why for Paul Jesus is not a wise man, or a new Moses with a new Law, or even the right interpretation of the old Law, as for Matthew. That would still be Law. In other words, redemption does not depend on what Jesus said and did or on our doing as he had said and done. Rather redemption depends on what God has done through Jesus' cross and resurrection — to bring on the New Age.

We can now see why Paul treats the theme of "Jesus and Judaism" in a highly dialectical way. On the one hand, for Paul the phrase "Jesus and Judaism" makes sense not only because he knows that Jesus was a Jew, but also because he believes that Jesus is the Christ, the Messiah, the one in whom God's promise to Israel was kept. On the other hand, Paul became convinced that this promise-keeping will extend the benefits (salvation) to the gentiles, because Christ's resurrection signalled the coming of the New Age for all creation. Those who believed that this has occurred and were made participants in Christ by baptism are redeemed from bondage to sin and death, whoever they may be. This redemption is not possible by obedience to Judaism's Law. Moreover, Paul knows that gentiles could become converts to Judaism (as in fact some did) and so become beneficiaries of God's promise to Abraham. But that would not redeem them from sin and death any more than being obedient to the Torah would redeem Jews. But by believing the good news about Jesus and being baptized, both Jew and gentile were redeemed, both made recipients of God's promise and both made real children of Abraham (Gal. 3:7, 14). Further, the fact that the Jesus-event occurred *in* Judaism does not make obedience to Judaism's Torah mandatory for all but the opposite: redemption now is through faith and baptism.

In other words, Paul offers us an entirely different way of thinking about Jesus' relation to Judaism. It is different not only from that of Matthew and John, but also from our own concern to see the significance of Jesus by locating him historically in Judaism. For Paul, one discerns the saving significance of Jesus by thinking through the meaning of the Jesus-event as a whole, in its relation to Israel and Scripture *and* in relation to the human condition. Theologically, I believe that Paul's way is best.

CONCLUSION

It is clear, to begin with, that none of the New Testament authors we have looked at is interested in presenting a fair, historically accurate picture of Jesus *in* Judaism. Instead, each in his own way is interested in distinguishing Jesus from Judaism while at the same time insisting that he was part of it. None of them suggests that Jesus' Jewishness is something that must be overcome. Of the three writers we noted, only Paul's interpretive framework would be congenial to a historically accurate picture of Jesus' relation to Judaism, because while the significance of Jesus for the human condition does not depend on an accurate historical account of Jesus' ministry, it is congenial with it. In the case of Matthew and John, however, insisting on a historically sound picture of Jesus in Judaism, as we understand it, would require a complete rewriting of their Gospels.

Must we, then, choose between a quest for an accurately reconstructed past (Jesus in Judaism) and the exegesis of the Gospels as we have them? By no means. Not if we think through the function of each of these enterprises.

I continue to believe that historically sound information about Jesus in Judaism is important not only with regard to Jewish-Christian relations, but even more with regard to the Christian community itself. Sound historical reconstruction of the past is a major way we have of testing all the things people say about Jesus. The conclusion of Matthew's Passion story suggests that he faced the same problem in his day. In any case, in our time we justify our own thought and action by appealing to Jesus — what he said and did, how he acted, and what he intended. A historically sound reconstruction of Jesus in Judaism is the only way we have of assessing whether these appeals are valid. For example, to justify our own revolutionary activity by appealing to Jesus the revolutionary is valid only if one can establish the probability that he was a revolutionary. In other words, we need the historical Jesus *in* Judaism to keep us honest.

Furthermore, keeping ourselves honest includes coming to terms with those elements of Matthew and John that are not historically accurate reports but that reflect the results of the growing tension between church and synagogue. That means coming to terms with our own past, with our own Christian history that forgot that the Matthean and Johannine picture had a particular historical context and is not constitutive of the gospel itself.

Interestingly enough, it is precisely the concern for our honesty and integrity that requires us also to interpret carefully the Gospels we have, which accent Jesus *and* Judaism. Why does Matthew, writing for a church that is increasingly gentile, emphasize so much the difference between Jesus and the Pharisees? It is not only to account for Jesus' execution. He also emphasizes Jesus' criticism of the Pharisees because he sees the same dangers within the church. In other words, for Matthew the abuses of Pharisaism that Jesus attacks lurk also in the Christian. To miss this not only distorts the past, but fosters illusions about ourselves.

Finally, the interpretive frameworks of John and Paul, while quite different, nonetheless show that the formulation "Jesus *and* Judaism" is essential theologically if the integrity of Christianity is to be preserved. What is at stake here is not only the truth about Jesus but the truth about ourselves. In John's case, it has to do with ourselves as creatures who prefer darkness to light because our deeds are evil (John 3:19). That insight is valid only because a Jesus who confronts us as radically as the Johannine Jesus confronted the Johannine Jews is able to provide the radical alternative we need. In Paul's case, it has to do with ourselves as enslaved to sin and death. To the extent to which that insight is valid, only a Jesus who is God's Act is able to redeem us. In this context what matters is not our agreement with John or Paul, but recognizing that an adequate theological grasp of the meaning of Jesus for salvation requires an interpretive framework that transcends what we usually mean by history.

NOTES

1. See Hans Dieter Betz, *Galatians*, Hermeneia Commentary (Philadelphia: Fortress Press, 1979), 79 n. 105, for references.

2. The allusion is to the title of Chester C. McCown's survey of the history of attempts to recover the Jesus of history from the Gospels and other evidence: *The Search for the Real Jesus* (New York: Charles Scribner's Sons, 1940).

3. E.g., Maurice Casey's study of the development of early Christology declares flatly, "It took some 50 or 60 years to turn a Jewish prophet into a Greek God" (*From Jewish Prophet to Gentile God* [Louisville: Westminster/John Knox Press, 1991], 97). See my review in *Interpretation* 47 (1993): 413–14.

4. Günther Bornkamm's influential *Jesus of Nazareth* (New York: Harper and Bros., 1960; German original 1956) is a convenient example of this misrepresentation. He compares Judaism with "a soil hardened and barren through its age-long history and tradition [i.e., legalism], yet a volcanic, eruptive ground, out of whose cracks and crevices breaks forth again and again the fire of a burning expectation [i.e., apocalypse]." They both have the same origin: "a faith in a God is beyond the world and history." Given God as distant in such a Judaism, the decisive, historically demonstrable difference in Jesus is that he makes God present. "There is nothing in contemporary Judaism which corresponds to the immediacy with which he teaches." In fact, "the reality of God and the authority of his will are always directly present, and are fulfilled in him" (55–56, 57). For an extensive critique, see my "Bornkamm's *Jesus of Nazareth* Revisited," *Journal of Religion* 49 (1969): 1–17. In the 10th, revised edition (not translated), Bornkamm acknowledged the force of my critique (*Jesus von Nazareth*, Urban Taschenbucher. [Stuttgart: Kohlhammer, 1975]; Nachwort, esp. 209–10) and observed that his intent was to express Jesus' own critique of Judaism, which admittedly offends Jews. Unfortunately, Bornkamm also claimed to be writing as a historian, and it is precisely the historian's view of Judaism that was made to serve apologetic interests.

5. This point is emphasized in my *A Future for the Historical Jesus* (Philadelphia: Fortress Press; rev. 2d. ed. 1981).

6. For an instructive discussion, see J. Andrew Overman, *Matthew's Gospel and Formative Judaism: The Social World of the Matthean Community* (Minneapolis: Fortress Press, 1990).

7. See Jack Dean Kingsbury, "The Developing Conflict between Jesus and the Jewish Leaders in Matthew's Gospel: A Literary-Critical Study," *Catholic Biblical Quarterly* 49 (1987): 57–73.

8. This is why Samuel Sandmel thinks that Matthew is appealing to Jews over the heads of the religious establishment. Sandmel, *Anti-Semitism in the New Testament?* (Philadelphia: Fortress Press, 1978), 69.

9. See the pathbreaking work by J. Louis Martyn, *History and Theology in the Fourth Gospel* (Nashville: Abingdon Press, 1968; 2d ed., 1979), followed by Raymond E. Brown, *The Community of the Beloved Disciple* (New York/Toronto: Paulist Press, 1979), which reconstructs the history of the Johannine community into the second century.

10. The impact of the Scrolls has been emphasized by James H. Charlesworth, "How the Dead Sea Scrolls Have Revolutionized Our Understanding of the Gospel of John," *Bible Review* 9 (1993): 27–38.

11. The New Testament contains thirteen letters that claim Paul as their author. Because of their differences in vocabulary, style, and content, few scholars today regard all of them as genuinely from Paul. There is, however, agreement that Romans, 1 and 2 Corinthians, Galatians, Philippians, 1 Thessalonians, and Philemon are genuine. There is wide, but not universal, agreement that 1 and 2 Timothy and Titus were written much later by a disciple of Paul. There is considerable disagreement over the genuineness of Ephesians, Colossians, and 2 Thessalonians.

Chapter 4

Christology: Unfinished Business

Hugh Anderson

From ancient times until now Christology has most frequently been construed as the attempt to search out and formulate an adequate theory or doctrine of the absoluteness of the being of Jesus Christ. Centuries of abstract thinking, rational argumentation, and propositional theologizing have been given to the project of articulating verbally how the divinity of Jesus is related to the transcendence of the God he dared to call Father and to his full participation in the human condition. The search to date we can hardly deem to have been conspicuously successful. That is not surprising. All christological statements, formulations, theories are the work of frail and fallible human witnesses, and not a single one can be regarded as final or complete or directly God-given. But even if a widely accepted theoretical solution to the mystery of the divinity-humanity of Jesus were ever to emerge, the question would at once arise: would it have any effect whatever in the lives of men and women in the churches, or even more so in the marketplace and on main street?

The rather vulgar word "business" in the title of this paper is used advisedly. It smacks of the earthy, the worldly, the marketplace and main street, and in a sense also of the life of the churches, where there is much talk of and pride in being engaged on church business, often, of course, with very little thought given to what its real business is. The term may accordingly serve to suggest what we shall seek to bring out later, that Christology, the question of the divinity of the human Jesus and his relation to the transcendent God, has never been merely a theoretical question, to be settled by logical argument. Rather is Christology intricately interwoven with the basic issues of faith or despair regarding the trustworthiness of ultimate Reality, of life and death or the way human beings conduct their lives in face of the one great certainty, death and its dark threat. The author of the Fourth Gospel sheds bright light on what we are saying here when he speaks of "doing the Truth." The great roll call of the faithful in the eleventh chapter of Hebrews also brilliantly illustrates the fact that all faith is essentially praxis (action). Martin Luther's dictum is true to the Scripture: "Faith is the doer and love the deed."

In my view it is incumbent on us in our secular age to try to show Christian believers and unbelievers alike that the Christology question is not simply a matter of esoteric debate (sadly often acrimonious) within the academy, but relates directly to the practical experience of men and women in their lived world. Are we to suppose then that theoretical discussion of the God-man problem, in its long and painful history, has been of no account or value? I think not. It has been of consuming interest for some of the greatest intellects from antiquity to the present. And if faith is the total response of humans to their being-in-the-world, then clearly their cognitive or rational faculty is involved, as well as the will or conscience or emotions, to say nothing at this point of the imagination. Even if our major submission will be that there is urgent need for us today to wed theory and praxis, it is no more than a truism to observe that in advocating our case we shall of necessity be engaged in the process of verbalizing it as best we can and of presenting what, we at least hope, will be logical arguments.

The subject-matter of Christology cannot be confined to such data as may be recovered and reconstructed by historical-critical inquiry concerning the life and person of the man Jesus of Nazareth. In jargon terms, Christology is more than "Jesusology." Of course, Jesus is the one who marks off the Christ-event from other events and imparts to it its distinctive character. We must recall, however, that in its totality the Christ-event reaches back to the covenants God made of old with his people Israel and forward into the history of the Christian community, with its priceless legacy of two thousand years of tradition, incorporating the Fathers of the church, the ancient creeds, councils, popes, the Reformers, later confessions, and theologians and thinkers of every period.

At this point it is necessary to add two cautionary comments. First, the Christ event, of which Jesus is the center, must not be submerged in the vast misty ocean of two millennia of church history, lest we lose sight of the so-called historical Jesus, and that in the fullness of his humanity, as we shall stress. Second, we have to recognize a salient and very significant difference between the ancient creeds of the church, such as Nicea and Chalcedon, for example, and the testimony of the New Testament to Jesus Christ. Following early church tradition and Christian writings both canonical and extra-canonical, the creeds seek to encapsulate within their brief compass a complete definition of the whole essence of Christian belief. Despite their continuing worth as vehicles of orthodox doctrine, they are couched in an abstract and static language of *substance* that is probably alien or obscure or even offensive to many people now. Notwithstanding the presence in the New Testament of kerygmatic and hymnic materials that are embryonically creedal (e.g., 1 Cor. 15:3–5; Phil. 2:5–11), the documents are for the most part transcripts of first-hand encounters with and experiences of Jesus Christ himself; and their writers give every impression not of trying to define their faith, but of being impelled by the dynamics of a living faith to grope for a language suitable to express the immensities of their experience.

The experiential or existential dimension in New Testament Christology or, if you like, its relationship to and implications for the human situation, is congenial to our emphasis on the necessity of wedding theory and praxis (action), and I think justifies us in according the primacy, for our christological reflection, to the New Testament. We do so, to be sure, not because of any pan-Protestant sentiment that would denigrate the significance of ecclesiastical tradition, and certainly not because of any Fundamentalist conviction that nothing outside of Scripture matters one whit, a view that is woefully reductionist and jejune and to that extent very damaging. Moreover I agree with Professor Keck that the obsession with the question of how it all began back in the first century of our era and the concomitant expectation, an illusory expectation, that a one-to-one relation between the man Jesus and his own self-consciousness and the church's belief in and preaching of Christ could be established by historical inquiry alone, has been counter-productive. Counter-productive in the sense that it obscures or negates altogether the mystery of God's *hiddenness* in the person, life, death, and resurrection of Christ and leaves precious little if any space for the emergence of new understandings in the ongoing history of the church. Preoccupation with the recovery of the "facts" of Jesus' life by strictly historical inquiry cannot by itself bring us to or guarantee for us the truth about the Christ of faith.

We stand then by our earlier statement that Christology is more than "Jesusology." Neither the long quest of the Jesus of history, nor research into the titles applied to him later has brought us to assured conclusions about the actual specifics of his life. The recent resurgence of Jesus Research, stimulated by remarkable archaeological discoveries in the land of Jesus and by intensive study of the large body of extra-biblical literature roughly contemporary with the New Testament writings, at best illumines the being and doing of Jesus himself only indirectly by illumining the cultural environment of the Galilee and Judea of his day.

However, in spite of our negative estimate of the significance of historico-critical investigation, we hasten to say that we dare not neglect the human Jesus nor the imaginative praxis of his ministry, the main lineaments of which, in my judgment, are still accessible to us, at least in a general way. The human Jesus is the principal clue to the character of the Christ-event. And in an age in which humankind's overriding concern is with the future shape of humanity, theologians like the Catholic priest-scholar Edward Schillebeeckx and a growing number of others are to be commended for maintaining that Christology must begin from below with the human Jesus, and that today we require a fresh vision of Jesus as the one who shows us the true meaning of humanity as well as its future goal, who liberates us, unites theory and praxis, and kindles the hope that an authentic disclosure-experience may emerge.

In a penetrating analysis of the critiques of religion by Feuerbach and Marx, Waite Willis rightly complains that their attacks, especially the latter's, were really leveled against the God of a traditional and obsolete theism, who is ensconced in high heaven and from that unimaginable distance promises eternal blessing to men and women, but actually abandons them to wretchedness on earth.[1] Authentic Trinitarian faith by contrast resolutely resists the separation of a wholly transcendent and impassive God from the creation and instead lives out of the power-in-weakness of "the God who concretely and sensuously gives himself to be known in the man Jesus as he acts on behalf of human suffering." But we would want to turn that around and claim that, in dealing with Christology, what needs to be asked is not how the divine can possibly become embodied in the human, since that inevitably removes us from the sphere of human imagination and praxis and commits us to the abstract and theoretical. Rather the mystery we have to ask about, and it is a mystery that cannot be resolved by the historian, armed even with the sharpest tools, is how the vulnerable human being Jesus of Nazareth, "a most ordinary man" in the terse and striking words of my Edinburgh University colleague James Mackey, can be encountered as the very nearness of God, as divine. Let me quote Mackey further: "The human creature, Jesus of Nazareth, accepted as such without any qualification, is where we start; not with any presence beside or behind him, betrayed by kinds of action which could not be human."[2]

Keeping the foregoing observations firmly in mind, and in particular our support of the practicalist thesis, we proceed now to consider three leading, representative approaches to the Christology question from the last two decades or so. Our concern is not with their historical veracity or the lack of it, but their theological viability. I name them respectively (1) the genetic or organic; (2) the kerygmatic; (3) the mythopoetic, which involves us in trying to articulate a theology of resurrection.

THE GENETIC OR ORGANIC

In his prize-winning monograph of 1977, *The Origin of Christology,* C. F. D. Moule propounds the thesis that "development" is a more suitable term than "evolution" for the genesis of Christology.[3] "Development" denotes an organic outgrowth from the parent stem, that is, the person of Jesus himself. To use the term "evolution" on the other hand would imply the intrusion into the gradual process of unfolding the meaning of the life and work of Jesus Christ of alien factors from the cultural environment of early Christianity. In short, as Moule has it, everything the church thought and said about Christ was fully present in Jesus from the very first.

The linchpin of this straight-line, substantial continuity between the human Jesus and the Christ accorded divine honors is the resurrection, by which Jesus becomes an eternally living being, possibly like the "spiritual body" of 1 Corinthians 15, and is constituted an inclusive Israel-wide or indeed Adam-wide corporate person, who can thus be described in terms appropriate to nothing less than God himself. Moule speaks several times of the resurrected Christ as *totally alive* or as possessed of absolute life.

Moule's account contains one or two valid insights. The tracing of an organic connection between the man Jesus and the church's Christology may serve as a safeguard of sorts against attempting to disengage the historical actualities of Jesus' earthly life from their mythological and theological framework, although of course Moule says nothing about mythology and too little about *theology*. Again, terms like "spirit-body" and "corporate person" employed by Moule, but not explicated further, are suggestive for the earthing or rooting of the church's Christology in its liturgy, worship, and praxis, as we shall subsequently note.

Nevertheless his position has serious weaknesses. He is still operating at the level of theory and abstraction. His aim is to define and demonstrate the absolute being of Jesus Christ. The focus is on the cosmic proportions of the Christ-figure, which are construed as being present in Jesus from the beginning. But the philosophy of history that lies behind all this is gravely flawed. Organic growth in the realm of nature is not an acceptable analogy to the intricacies and complexities of historical movement or process. In the field of history, "the sphere of the human" according to Ernst Troeltsch, many a curve-ball, or in cricket terminology many a googly, is thrown: there are departures from base, unexpected deviations and mutations. Or, to put it another way, human beings and their modes of understanding are not like a river of water flowing in one direction between well-defined banks. Shifts in cultural environment do inevitably give rise to shifts in perception of the truth or truths experienced as formative or trans-formative for people's lives. The rich variety of Christologies in the New Testament, the numerous attempts to label Jesus by the attribution to him of different titular dignities (each one singly and all collectively inadequate vehicles), should provide the *coup de grâce* to Moule's rather deterministic theory.

Whereas he strives zealously to uphold the decisive centrality of the man Jesus for the church's Christology, in the book we are discussing at least, Moule really tells us nothing about the human Jesus, about his message of the kingdom of God in its altogether surprising power of evocation and transformation, and in its pragmatic oneness with his death on the cross. In fact he deals only secondarily with the death of Christ and takes the event of the resurrection as the proper starting point of Christology. The climactic importance of the Easter story is not to be denied, but I shall argue that we miss its true force and meaning if we do not start with the death of Jesus. It is quite astonishing that Moule excludes the Gospels of Matthew, Mark, and Luke from his purview on the ground that they deal with how Jesus looked to observers *before* his death and so should not be called in to testify about post-Easter experience. But is it not a commonplace that all four canonical Gospels are written from faith to faith and enshrine within them allusions to Jesus' public ministry *and* the interpretative perspectives of the followers of Christ in the early church?

To sum up: the chief flaw in Moule's hypothesis is that, in its preoccupation with the being of Christ *as he was in himself*, it misses almost entirely the relational aspect of human history (though he does give it a passing nod), the very fabric of which is the impact and responses of persons toward one another, of encounter and encounter as acted upon. We have to remember in any case that all claims for the absoluteness of Christ's being, whether we think of them as stemming from the Bible, from the theologian, or indeed from the ordinary believer, are ultimately *human* claims. The real test of the validity of the Christ idea is not its theoretical appeal to reason or logic, but how the divine-human Jesus Christ is experienced by men and women and the effect that has on their lives.

THE KERYGMATIC

In response to Rudolf Bultmann's historical negativism and his
much controverted assertion that the Jesus of history was only
one presupposition among others for Christian theology, the so-
called "New Quest" of the earthly Jesus came to life in the 1950s
and was carried on into the 1960s. Its exponents set themselves
the task of building the bridge between the man Jesus and the
Christ of the church's kerygma or preaching, of exploring how
Jesus the proclaimer of the reign of God was related to the
Christ proclaimed in the church's gospel. Günther Bornkamm,
for instance, in raising afresh the question of the historical
Jesus, intimated that he was looking for the kerygma in the
mission and message of Jesus and for Jesus in the church's
kerygma.[4]

The "New Quest" thus construed passed into limbo relatively quickly. The probable reasons for that we can only
briefly mention here: the decline of the existentialist theology,
which the German scholars still shared with their teacher, Bultmann; sensitivity to the fact that theology (or existentialist
philosophy) and history were strangely fused together so that
theological presuppositions dictated or predetermined historical judgments; the advance of new modes of criticism, largely
literary (structuralist, theoretical, symbolic, and so forth), with
the accompanying conviction that ancient texts and the interpretation of them were in no sense dependent upon the
historian's reconstruction of their first contextual setting.

I have, however, its defects notwithstanding, included the
kerygmatic standpoint of the "New Quest" in this essay, because it gave expression to two basic perceptions that are
indispensable to a fuller grasp of New Testament Christology.
First, even if we err, as we surely do, in thinking that the bridge
between the man Jesus and the church's gospel of Christ can be
built, and be shown to be built, by historical-critical engineer-
ing, from a theological perspective we must not relinquish the
connection or continuity between the two. Much modern theology has done just that. Liberal Protestant theology, culminating
in Harnack, isolated Jesus of Nazareth from the developed
Christology of the church and held that the essence of Christianity lay in Jesus' message of the kingdom of God, understood
as an ethic of the Fatherhood of God and the brotherhood of

man. On the other hand the influential neo-orthodox theology, with its thoroughgoing christocentrism and its emphasis on soteriology, reduced the human Jesus to a vanishing point.

Second, another merit of the "New Quest" was the way it handled the christological titles: Messiah, Lord, Son of God, Son of Man, Suffering Servant, and so forth. No doubt each of the titles represents a particular label placed upon Jesus by one group or another among the early Christian communities. But none of them singly nor all of them together can offer a comprehensive definition of the life and person of Christ. That holds good even if it could ever be proven, which is highly unlikely, given the inconclusive results of the voluminous literature on the subject *to date,* that *not the church but Jesus* thought of himself as the Son of Man. The mystery of the hidden presence of God in the words and deeds of Jesus is beyond the scope of the titles: probably that is why there are so many in the New Testament. Accordingly we welcome the way in which practitioners of the "New Quest" (and other theologians, it must be added) have consigned the christological titles to the margin as links in the chain between the human Jesus and the Christ of the church's preaching. They have turned instead to other facts of Jesus' ministry, his teaching on the kingdom of God, his healings with their declarations of forgiveness, his rejection of the establishment and his turning instead to the poor, the outcasts, and the dispossessed, his own decision of faith, and his death on the cross in obedience to the will of God. In such words and deeds inhered the secret of his oneness with God. That secret, during the course of his public ministry, was discernible, of course, only to those who had the eyes to see and the ears to hear. After Jesus' death his followers sought in their Christologies to make it an "open secret," but even then it remained closed to all those who could not contemplate or tolerate the oneness with God of an ordinary man put to death on a Roman cross.

THE MYTHOPOETIC APPROACH, AND THE NEED FOR AN APPROPRIATE THEOLOGY OF RESURRECTION

The term "mythopoetic" demands some explanation. The recognition since D. F. Strauss, and more so of late since Bultmann,

that the New Testament is permeated by myth, can be considered a positive gain to its interpretation. But the fact is that a
great majority of professing Christians in every branch of the
church are hostile to the concept of myth and gravely suspect
the integrity of anyone who ventures to uphold the prominence
of the mythological element in the Bible. Literal-minded as they
are, they feel that to characterize biblical reports or stories as
mythical is really to dismiss them as *untrue*. Since for them
myth and history are indistinguishable from each other, they
accept *all* biblical statements at face value as reporting bare facts
accurately and indeed mathematically. But should we not have
learned, from the infliction upon our youth of the weariness of
the flesh that was schoolbook history, that a mere assemblage
of facts in and by itself has no power to touch or affect our
existence or the way we live at the deeper level? The mythological element in the Bible, for instance, the pictorializing of
a higher world above and beyond our own, in which human
destinies are shaped, is scarcely acceptable as fact today, at any
rate where the rational faculty is allowed its place. Yet it has the
capacity to move us out beyond sensory perception to the mystery of the Trans-human, the Transcendent. Or, if we translate
the myth in existentialist terms, the capacity to bring us into
touch with the ultimate Reality, which is the ground of all our
beings!

Now myth and poetry are the closest of allies. As modes
of communication, neither is at all dependent on the presentation of hard facts. The truth of both belongs not to the material
facts or supposed facts contained in them or lying behind them,
but is the truth of the creative imagination, of emotion and experience, of religious feeling. Influenced by the rise of Higher
Criticism, in the late nineteenth century Matthew Arnold re-
acted strongly against the biblical fundamentalism opposed to
it. He was persuaded that a type of discourse, which was not
necessarily true in a factual or scientific way, constituted an in-
valuable dynamic for the renewing, vitalizing, and ennobling
of a society or civilization. Therefore he believed that the Bible
could be rescued only by accepting the poetic nature of its
language and subsuming it under the heading of poetry. Is it
not intriguing, if somewhat ironical, that a hundred years after
Arnold we are still struggling might and main to save the Bible
from the clutches of the literalists whose passionate attachment

to hard facts quite overwhelms the much profounder appeal of
the biblical poetics to the creative imagination?

Let us now (as briefly as possible) apply these general
considerations to the New Testament, principally the Gospels.

Of the four Gospels, only Mark's does not enclose the story
of Jesus' public ministry within a framework consisting on the
one side of infancy narratives, as in Matthew and Luke, or of a
hymnic prologue to the Logos or Word become flesh, as in the
case of John, and on the other side of dramatic, concrete stories
of the resurrection of Christ and of the appearance(s) of Jesus
to his disciples. This holds good for Mark, of course, only if we
assume, as I think we should, that his Gospel ends at 16:8, with
the women running from the tomb in silent fear of the holy, the
numinous, and so contains no appearance story. What then are
we to make of the predictions of Christ's passion, death, and
resurrection in Mark 9:31 and 10:33? In their precise detail, particularly 10:33, they are almost certainly prophecies after the
event retrojected onto the lips of Jesus. But even as such, we
need to consider them as integral parts of Mark's Gospel *as a
whole*. The salient theme running throughout is the lowly way of
Jesus under the suspicious eyes of the authorities, and so under
the shadow of the cross from the beginning, to his actual death
on Calvary. Face-on with the crucified one in the moment of his
death, a Roman centurion, of all people, confessed: "Truly this
man was the Son of God" (Mark 15:39). Obviously he needed
no additional event beyond Christ's death to elicit his belief
or faith. So the predictions of Christ's rising again in Mark
9:31 and 10:33 should be construed not as documentation of a
separate miraculous event, but as indicators of the redemptive
efficacy of his death. We have something analogous in John's
use of the verb *hypsothēnai*, which denotes both Christ's being
lifted up on the cross and his amazing closeness to God *in that
death* for those who can endure the thought.

Perhaps then Mark's Gospel offers us the surest clue as to
how we should interpret the mythopoetic framework in which
the story of Jesus' life and death is encased in the other Gospels.
The bulk of the birth stories and the Easter texts is in prose.
But who would care to deny their overall poetic quality? Here
most assuredly a dull, prosaic, and unimaginative literalism is
totally unable to plumb the depths. In the first two chapters of
Luke the poetic surfaces openly in the odes, psalms, or songs

of the Magnificat, the Benedictus, and Nunc Dimittis. But there is also the poetic symbolism of the idyll of the shepherds and the heavenly chorus of angels, facts or events of an ancient age neither of them! In the second chapter of Matthew, the visit of the Magi picturesquely symbolizes the entry of the gentiles into the Christian fold, reminiscent as it is of the Queen of Sheba's visit to King Solomon in 1 Kings 10:1–10: "Blessed be the Lord your God, who has delighted in you and set you on the throne of Israel!... Then she gave the king a hundred and twenty talents of gold, and a very great quantity of spices and precious stones; never again came such an abundance of spices as these which the queen of Sheba gave to Solomon."

The infancy narratives, or rather the mythopoetic language in which they are expressed, directly conveys to the reader's imagination "theatrical materials" for the Incarnation: the term "theatrical materials" is justified by centuries of Christian art and architecture, iconography and drama, poetry and hymnology. The language in itself mediates a vision of the entire creation waiting with shimmering expectation for the arrival of a new day of God. But even more importantly it communicates the experience of the early followers of Jesus of the transforming presence of the divine spirit in and through that most ordinary man, born of a Jewish woman in the lowliest of locations. The obscurity of Jesus' birth, and it is obscure beyond the historian's reach, corresponds extremely well with the perpetual obscurity to which the powers of this world would fain have consigned him by crucifying him on a Roman gibbet.

Likewise the Easter reports are not to be regarded as furnishing documentary evidence of an actual past event. The language of the Easter stories, in spite of or, perhaps better, because of their concreteness, is itself the mythopoetic vehicle of expression of feelings on the part of the disciples that lie too deep for tears or laughter: feelings that the divine spirit had invaded their lives, to their re-creation, through their encounter with the self-giving death of Jesus, perfectly consistent as it was with his self-giving to the poor and needy in the course of his ministry. The God with whom Jesus had confronted them in his largely parabolic speech, therefore the *hidden* God whom they barely comprehended, was now vindicated, in his hidden involvement in Christ's sacrificial death, as *the* God who had opened up for them a new country. Only now, through death's undoing in death and all that it meant in their experience, they could not name their God without in the same breath naming the name of Jesus, that is to say, without confessing the divinity of the man on the cross.

I am, to be sure, very well aware that the vast majority of people consider even the slightest hint that the resurrection of Christ was not a historical event separate from the death of Jesus to be anathema, or as some have learned to their cost, the cause of considerable personal rancor. The customary rejoinder to any such suggestion is the assertion that it *must* have taken the miraculous event of the physical reappearance of Christ to accomplish the metamorphosis of the first followers from their craven cowardice to the mood of buoyancy and irrepressible joy, which impelled them to promulgate the "good news." So the explanation of the accounts of Easter, widely accepted by both scholars and members of the church at large, is that Christ did rise in bodily form from the grave (many would add in the form of a spiritual body, if anyone could possibly conceive what that might be), and that his appearances to his followers are proof positive of the reality of that event. The event is generally taken to be an act of God, an event "without parallel." And at the popular level it is frequently held that God could, of course, work any miracle he wanted for his son.

Now there is a certain plausibility in that standpoint, inasmuch as it accords priority to Jesus over against the subjective inner feelings or experiences of the disciples themselves. But it is not above criticism or altogether incontestable. Let us take objection at once to the simplistic notion that God could perform any miracle he pleased in and through his son. Surely the Father God of Jesus does not overwhelm the humanity of Jesus or any of his children by using them arbitrarily as media for the manifestation of his miraculous power, like a Russian chessmaster displaying his prowess by lifting and placing the pawns in the game. Again, the resurrection cannot simply be the resuscitation of a dead body. If it were no more than that, then Jesus would be no different from the once dead Lazarus, raised but still bound in his grave-clothes and doomed to die again. Theologians have tried to refine the crassness of any theory of resuscitation by describing the Easter event as unique, and uniquely God's own doing. But if the resurrection is a unique event, without analogy in human experience, can we regard it as a real event at all in any received sense of the word? It has to be added also that the sheer physical proximity of another person, good and true and just and selfless, is in itself no guarantee that those who encounter such a one will be inspired to a like virtue. During his earthly ministry people close to Jesus could attack him as operating by the hand of Beelzebul or the devil. By the same token faith, that is, the trusting response of men and women to the coherence and integrity of ultimate reality, cannot be made to depend on the physical proximity of the resurrected Christ. We remember the dramatic denouement of the Emmaus story in Luke 24, reminiscent of the *anagnorisis*, or recognition scene, in Greek tragedy: "Their [the two disciples'] eyes were opened and they knew him, *and he vanished out of their sight.*" John concludes his Easter stories with the liberating pronouncement of 20:29: "Jesus said to Thomas, 'Have you believed because you have seen me? Blessed are those who have not seen and yet believe.'"

What the first disciples and all human beings ever since have seen and known is the inescapable reality or event-character of death itself. When we sit by the bedside of a terminally ill friend, what moves us to the very depths of our being is not in these moments the expectation of life hereafter. It is assuredly perfectly natural and human to hope and long for life beyond death for those we have loved. We still clutch "the unconquerable hope," still nurse "the inviolable shade." But it is at once the sadness and grandeur of our existence that we do not know, we have no proof of what lies beyond the "bourne from which no traveler returns." Our dead have not come back in the body to tell us: only as out of the secret places of the most high God have they come to us in the silence of their *spiritual* closeness bringing us a benediction of peace and tranquillity.

In the company of the terminally ill we are overtaken by the extraordinary gallantry with which ordinary people endure suffering and accept the inevitability of the grim Reaper's advent. In nearness to the dying we experience a kind of *frisson*, or shuddering, as if the Divine Spirit were seeking to break through to us, arming us against the last great certainty, our own death, and reminding us that the clear realization of our mortality enriches our depth perception of all things living. In "Sunday Morning" the American agnostic poet Wallace Stevens writes:

> Death is the mother of beauty, hence
> from her, Alone, shall come fulfilment
> to our dreams And our desires.

When the Apostle Paul depicts death as "the last enemy," he does not give his sanction to treat it as the final obscenity (as so often we do nowadays), which we should try to cheat by cosmeticizing it. In good Jewish fashion, Paul regards it as the termination of God's good gift of life. But as the last enemy, death is not merely the terminus to every human life, to be overcome in the next world by resurrection. Death prowls around our present world and lays its icy grip upon us day by ordinary day wherever in our immediate environment, or anywhere in the global village, oppression annihilates freedom, injustice triumphs over justice, falsehood over truth, and lovelessness over love.

Now the church is the body of Christ, and therefore inescapably, where it truly recognizes who its divine Lord is, his crucified body. If it is not impelled, as his body, by its praxis and liturgy to reach outward to the reversing of the tragic death-process we have just spoken of and the mending of a broken world, Christ is still captive in the grave: his body remains sorely wounded insofar as its members are not open to the enabling power of God's spirit and spurn the grace offered to them through the experienced renewal in their midst of the presence of Jesus in his life and through his death. In brief, where Christian believers have opportunity to improve the human condition, and yet death is somehow permitted to stalk all around them in life, by oppression, injustice, falsehood, and lovelessness, then we can say that Jesus is not risen.

Notice has often been taken of the quite distinct echoes in the most arresting Easter stories of the church's fellowship meal, the Lord's Supper or the Eucharist. Nowhere more distinct than in the climax of the Emmaus story in Luke 24, where Jesus is known at last for who he truly is, the ordinary yet strange man who embraced the pain and seeming Godforsakenness of the cross in utter fidelity to the will of that silent and hidden God who sent no legion of angels to save him! "Was it not necessary that the Christ should suffer these things and enter into his glory?" (Luke 24:26). In the church's praxis the celebration of the Lord's Supper is not merely a summons to remember an abhorrent event of the distant past. Neither is the reading of the resurrection stories in the celebration of Easter a call to a faith that can be founded in a rather nebulous event, of the faraway and long ago, whose traces are now irretrievably blotted out in the sands of time.

As media of the church's experience and confession of the divinity of Jesus, the concrete Easter stories find their proper place (in their harmony and unity with the incarnation) within the church's worship, not only in the Eucharist, to be sure, but certainly most significantly there. In the Pauline formula of institution (1 Cor. 11:24: "This is my body which is broken for you; this do in remembrance of me"), the liturgical imperative is not merely a request to memorialize the death of Christ. The word *anamnesis* ("remembrance") means "recapitulation," the actualization ever and afresh of the presence of the divine spirit that motivated Jesus' own living and dying. An authentic eucharistic praxis occurs where the participants are "inspired" by the conviction that death in the midst of our lives is defeated by a kind of dying. A dying to self and a turning toward the others in need, "inspired" by the vividly experienced self-offering of Christ in his life and death! Through the bread broken and the wine poured out, freely and gladly given and freely and gladly received, the crucified body and the shed blood of Jesus become the channel of the spirit's power, open the gates of new life for believers; death is undone by death and Jesus is truly risen.

In a poem entitled "The Transfiguration," the Scottish poet Edwin Muir conjures up a wonderfully evocative picture of the world and all creatures restored to their pristine state through Christ's having become "uncrucified." Of course in the poet's imagination, in order to be uncrucified, Christ had to be the one who once-for-all took up within himself in his death the world's sorrow and anguish.

> But he will come again, it's said, though not
> Unwanted and unsummoned; for all things,
> Beasts of the field, and woods, and rocks, and seas,
> And all mankind from end to end of the earth
> Will call him with one voice. In our own time,
> Some say, or at a time when time is ripe.
> Then he will come, Christ the uncrucified,
> His agony unmade, his cross dismantled —
> Glad to be so — and the tormented wood

Will cure its hurt and grow into a tree.
In a green springing corner of young Eden,
And Judas damned take his long journey backward
From darkness into light and be a child
Beside his mother's knee, and the betrayal
Be quite undone and never more be done.[5]

Jesus comes again "in our time" and, I submit, not in some far-off and unknown future "when time is ripe," when his sacrificial death becomes the spur to the conquest of death in life by the practice among believers of the self-giving and redeeming love that incredibly will not shut out even the Judases of history from a return to the Creator's Edenic intention for all his creatures. Therefore, in a darkening world like ours today, Christology is related to life's harsh realities, and it truly is as yet unfinished business.

I am well aware that the theology of resurrection for which I have argued requires much more extensive treatment, with detailed exegesis of the many relevant texts. But I trust I may have encouraged a rethinking of what the resurrection of Christ signifies and of the elemental part it plays in the church's Christology.

NOTES

1. *Theism, Atheism, and the Doctrine of the Trinity: The Trinitarian Theologies of Karl Barth and Jürgen Moltmann in Response to Protest Atheism* (Atlanta: Scholars Press, 1987).

2. See his *Jesus the Man and the Myth: A Contemporary Christology* (London: SCM Press, 1979). Mackey insists on a Christology that begins with the "human creature, Jesus of Nazareth."

3. Cambridge: Cambridge University Press, 1977.

4. In *Jesus of Nazareth*, trans. Irene and Fraser McLuskey with James M. Robinson (New York: Harper, 1960).

5. Quoted in David Daiches, *God and the Poets* (Oxford: Clarendon Press, 1984), 183.

Conclusion

Walter P. Weaver

Conclusions in theology are not easy to come by — at least ones acquiring universal assent. It is no different in the case of the works in this volume. Nevertheless, certain themes recur and compete for attention. To the delineation of these I direct this final essay.

First among them is the observation of a surging new interest in the historical Jesus.[1] A certain drought of concern has pervaded biblical studies since the Bultmannian domination, but a new era of interest has arisen. This interest is stirring among those whose focus lies simply in the historical problem itself,[2] or who care primarily about the theological matters that arise from consideration of the historical issues. I count myself among the latter, though certainly no one can travel through the theological jungle without having first traversed the historical desert.

Among the contributors Prof. Charlesworth is most conspicuously carrying the banner of the historians. Some years ago Ernst Käsemann remarked that someone needs to administer the estate of the historians,[3] and Charlesworth is notably moving along that path. He does so in a provocative and often new way, however, and certainly in the consciousness of one who has paid attention to his predecessors. In his oral response to Hugh Anderson's paper, Charlesworth noted, in a manner disclaiming the usual insistence of dialectical theology:

> My one problem is the constant appeal to some assured aspect
> of Jesus' historical existence, but at the same time the rejection
> of any possible dependence by faith on any conclusion from
> historical research. It seems to me the umbilical cord between
> historical research and Christian faith cannot be cut; the mys-
> tery weds the two together.... Christology must begin with the
> human Jesus, and that means there must be some minimal,
> unassailable facts.

Of course, just how many "unassailable facts" are necessary and
exactly what they are remain open for debate. Bultmann's *dass*
comes to mind here. Presumably the obvious answer would be:
as many facts as we can get, of whatever nature.

In the same vein Charlesworth's own foray into the "self-
understanding" of the Righteous Teacher and that of Jesus
drew some critical notice. This essay, in a quite original way,
draws upon the material from the Dead Sea Scrolls to raise a
comparison between the self-understanding of the Qumran
Teacher and Jesus. It makes its analogical case with coherence and persuasion, though both Anderson and I wondered
whether Charlesworth's use of the term "self-understanding"
did not, in fact, sound suspiciously like *Selbstbewusstein*. The
Heidegger-Bultmann school regarded self-consciousness as a
psychological term, implying some insight into what Jesus
consciously thought about himself, his messianic consciousness. Self-understanding, on the other hand, meant essentially
"understanding of existence," how the self is constituted, which
can be derived from one's deeds and words, but may not ever
necessarily be apparent in someone's self-consciousness. Self-
understanding can be hypothesized from intentionality, what a
subject seemingly intends, as seen again in word and deed.
Again, in the discussion following his paper Charlesworth
vigorously denied any intention on his part to probe Jesus'
self-consciousness:

> We cannot psychoanalyze or put Jesus on a couch. I have no
> interest at all in pursuing his self-consciousness. That's bad the-
> ology. It's also horrifying methodology.... To talk about Jesus'
> self-understanding is forced upon me because of the primary
> data, not because of any theological concern.

The denial is emphatic, but it is not yet so obvious why this
"self-understanding" is so different, when one after all argues

that in the Parable of the Wicked Workers Jesus speaks of the son and is referring to himself. Even if it is assumed that "son" here does not imply anything ontological, are we not jumping into Jesus' *consciousness* by supposing that he was talking about *himself?*[4] He could, after all, have been referring to anyone or no one in particular, even supposing that this element does go back to Jesus. We could also say, with Hugh Anderson:

> I'm not sure that what one thinks of one's self is in the last analysis the crucial thing. It is what one does and says and certainly out of what one does and says we can gather to some extent the character, the self-understanding, the intention, the aim, and the goal of the person involved.

Whether this kind of information is validly available from the synoptic material is subject to the usual disputes. Perhaps the discussion showed simply that a more precise definition of terminology is needed. Charlesworth's *Jesus within Judaism* discussed his intention in some more detail, indicating a use of "self-understanding" in a sense resembling "self-interpretation."[5] This self-interpretation certainly bears no relation to those older efforts to psychoanalyze Jesus but in actual practice still seems difficult to distinguish from many old-quest-style probings into Jesus' "self-consciousness."

In any case, there is an obvious new vigor in pursuing questions about the historical Jesus,[6] though it strikes me that, in scanning the literature, there exists a rather wide difference in evaluation of the evidence for reconstructing the picture. The images run from Marcus Borg's charismatic sage,[7] who looks a bit like a sixtyish social crusader, on through E. P. Sanders's prophet of eschatological restoration,[8] who bears at least a familial resemblance to Schweitzer's apocalyptic visionary, to Burton Mack's astonishing reconstruction of Christian origins,[9] which includes a summary of Jesus' public activity as an itinerant Cynic preacher, and to Dominic Crossan's similar characterization of Jesus as a Cynic Jewish peasant.[10] Yet there are common lines in all the pictures, suggesting that perhaps we ought not to overplay the differences either.

At the same time what appears to be most noticeable about this activity is not simply its diversity, but the revisioning process that it represents. One such revisionary tendency, for example, seems to be a movement toward dismantling of the apocalyptic Jesus.[11] The eschatological element is not denied, but the picture to which many of us had grown accustomed, of an apocalyptically excited Jesus running about in expectation of the imminent End, is being subjected to some serious questioning. Similarly, the idea of the historical Jesus as one who contested the Law, aroused opposition for his gracious treatment of sinners, and endured the hostility of Pharisees, also is experiencing some revision. This process occurs as newer understandings of the Judaism of Jesus' day have come available. A good instance is E. P. Sanders's Jesus-figure, who certainly held to the expectation of the kingdom and himself as King, but at the same time conducted no campaigns against the Law or, for that matter, against little in Judaism that might suggest hostility and got himself killed largely for overturning a few tables in the Temple.

It is always the case that every new generation of scholarship mounts its future on the shoulders of the preceding one, i.e., each generation has to take apart the previous consensus in order to make progress. In matters biblical and theological, this is especially the case, because the subject matter remains unchanged across the years. There may be newer discoveries, such as the Dead Sea Scrolls or the Nag Hammadi materials, which enhance knowledge of the historical circumstances, but the essential subject matter does not change. Biblical studies, including the whole question of the historical Jesus, remain a matter of reassessing the old picture, and perhaps adding new illumination cast on the environment through additional resources. The ultimate goal is to cast more clarifying light on the understanding of origins and especially of texts produced by movements. It could also be said that the goal of that goal is ultimately self-understanding in the sense of understanding of existence.

•

Problems of the historical Jesus abound and the historians will go on rehashing them and reevaluating as the evidence dictates. Beyond that lies the question of meaning for the community of faith. Given some information about the Jesus of history, we still ask of what significance it is for faith. What can we make of what we know about Jesus? Of course, no one has to be both-

ered about this question in order to have an interest in Jesus
as a powerful figure of history, and another characteristic of
the present time in "Jesus Research" is its fastening onto this
question without any visible commitments of faith. That likely
goes hand in hand with the fact that so much of biblical studies has migrated out of seminaries and into public institutions,
where especially the need is strong to demonstrate one's right
to exist in the academy as a respectable discipline. Securing this
right has been something of a struggle for departments of religion over a period of the last two or three decades, so it is
quite understandable that a posture of theological neutrality is
insisted on. (Whether an accompanying "objectivity" is actually
possible is quite another question.)

What all this seems to mean is that there exists still a pronounced separation of the historical Jesus from the Christ of
faith. And there is no universally agreed necessity to get them
together again. Certainly anyone who cares to is free to pursue
this question, but the interest in the Jesus of history, however
peculiar or quaint or weird or erratic he might have been, can
be cultivated entirely apart from the evaluations of faith. This
suggests that, in a way exceeding Bonhoeffer's vision, we have
"come of age" and can now face frontally, without so much as a
twitch, the honest-to-god truth about Jesus of Nazareth without
regard to the theological consequences. The situation suggests,
in fact, that an ever-deepening rift between the academy and
the church exists, that the church no longer controls its own
tradition, much less the academy.[12]

This separation between the Jesus of history and the Christ
of faith seems to parallel the separation between the academy
and the church. The Jesus of history, after all, is the historian's Jesus, the one who is "resurrected" by the methods of
historical criticism. The Christ of faith seems to be the province
of the church "out there" somewhere, and the divide between
them is permanently fixed, with no one in either camp com-
plaining. The historians can go on doing their thing and the
church people theirs, so long as the one knows not what the
other does. When occasionally a visitor sallies forth from his
castle in academia and instructs the *hoi polloi*, an outcry arises.[13]
Indignation is often aroused, though in short order the public
appetite for controversy is quickly turned to another subject.
Or in any event the local keepers of the church peace manage

to quiet the ruckus, at least until another iconoclast from the academy escapes his keepers and flees the zoo into the land of supposed reality.

Overdrawn, I hear it said, and certainly there is some planting of tongue in cheek. Yet, seriously, it was concern with this question of meaning, or theological value, that motivated my own essay. I proposed that we ought to think of the historical Jesus as a Parable, and that his story, as reconstructed precisely by historians, could well serve the interests of faith when conceptualized parabolically. This proposal aroused a number of questions, one of which was whether I was not, in fact, ontologizing metaphor, and therefore engaging in a kind of absolutizing of something that I had already claimed was actually quite relative.

That would be true if I had proposed to regard the Parable as permanently fixed, but, of course, it is not, and, in the nature of things, never can be. The actual content of the Parable will vary, as everyone knows who has read Schweitzer. I do not regard that as such a loss, since all theological statements are relative, including the one that asks for a response to the Easter kerygma. In any event, if Jesus is truly Parable, and if parable is truly metaphor, then theologically it can be said that God has ontologized metaphor. And I would not have any problem with that.

Other questions — not unfamiliar ones in this area — were raised regarding the relationship of faith and history and whether there is any necessary connection between the Jesus of history and the Christ of faith. My insistence that the two belong together brought forth the question of whether an encounter with the historical figure would then mean an encounter with the kerygmatic Christ. I stand by my response:

> I do think that discovering the historical Jesus, meaning the historian's Jesus, poses the question about the kerygmatic Christ. In other words, I think that coming up against the Jesus of history does not in any sense reduce the decision of faith; it doesn't make it any easier, probably makes it harder, but in that sense it also brings out the scandal involved in deciding whether just this Jesus is really of some ultimate significance.

The essay by Leander Keck also moved within the orbit of christological concern. His insightful journey through various New Testament conceptualities (Matthew, John, Paul) of the relation of Jesus to Judaism focused in a significant way the kinds of theological evaluations to be made of Jesus. Matthew's Jesus finds definition — and gives it to his community — primarily over against Judaism, with little attention to the continuities; John's Jesus puts the reader in the same theological (not historical) situation as the original "Jews": that of facing the question of whether just this Jesus is primally significant. Paul takes quite a different tack in that he betrays no real "historical" concern to see Jesus within Judaism, but only to reflect on the triangle of Christ-event, Israel, and the human condition.

It is interesting that, after this survey, Keck offers us the judgment that the Pauline way is best and that it is, in fact, most compatible with an interest in the historical Jesus in the modern sense. So we have here the paradoxical notion that the figure with seemingly the least interest in the "historical" Jesus represents the best theological perspective from which to engage in research into the Jesus of history. That seems to mean that only one who sees that he or she has no ultimate stake in the question, in terms of salvation, can engage the issue with a good conscience. Certainly Keck acknowledges the importance of Jesus Research; it provides the test by which many other competing voices can be measured. At the same time what ultimately counts is that which addresses the human condition; and Paul, above all, has seen most profoundly into that problem (echoes of Luther perhaps). In this regard Keck's final statement proved provocative:

> ... what matters is not our agreement with John or Paul, but the recognition that an adequate theological grasp of the meaning of Jesus for salvation requires an interpretive framework that transcends what we usually mean by history.

Presumably the Pauline interpretive framework is a conspicuous example of such a framework, but whether it transcends history as we understand it, i.e., as historically-critically reconstructed, may be left for further pondering, since even the Pauline framework becomes accessible to us only through that same critical methodology.

The essay by Hugh Anderson also directed attention — in a most extraordinarily literate way — to the question of how doing Christology must ultimately come down to "doing" life itself, that the "business" of Christology remains unfinished just so long as there remain the poor and oppressed in the world. This point was summarized by Keck as the main thesis of the essay:

> The real test of the validity of the Christ idea is not in its theoretical appeal to reason or logic, but how the divine-human Christ is experienced by men and women and the effect that has on their lives.

At the same time Keck observed the need for some "criteria to distinguish the spirits," i.e., some ways in which we tell whether the effect on someone's life comes from the spirit of Christ or from some other spirit, especially as so many things go around these days precisely in the name of Christ.

It is clear that Anderson is concerned to move the historic debate over Christology away from its moorings in ancient substantialist categories and into something graspable in the contemporary scene. He invites us to think of the New Testament language about Jesus the crucified-risen Christ as the mythopoetic expression of a real "something" rooted in the universal experience of comfort-in-face-of-death; "resurrection" cannot be a literal story of resuscitation, but the mirroring of this self-recovery before death itself. So also it is the coming to terms with the crucified one that inspires resurrection, and that happens only where the body of this crucified one, his church, finds itself engaged in the world in life-giving work. Such activity is symbolized for Anderson in the church's own sacramental life, where especially occurs the meeting with the crucified one. Something like a "demythologized" resurrection occurs in this Christology, without the encumbrances of an existentialist framework. This insistence also on a union of theory and praxis in undertaking the christological task is refreshingly commendable. Whether the term "myth" can itself be adequately sustained these days is, as Anderson knows, a matter of some contention. That he and I come together in seeking some other terminology for depicting the variegated language of the New Testament is also clear. Whether we have done so successfully must remain some of the "unfinished business" before us.[14]

NOTES

1. E.g., see the pertinent essays in E. P. Sanders, *Jesus and Judaism* (Philadelphia: Fortress Press, 1985); James H. Charlesworth, *Jesus within Judaism: New Light from Exciting Archaeological Discoveries* (New York: Doubleday, 1988); Marcus Borg, *Jesus: a New Vision* (San Francisco: Harper, 1987).

2. E.g., Sanders, who asserts (*Jesus and Judaism*, p. 2) "I am interested in the debate about the significance of the historical Jesus for theology in the way one is interested in something that he once found fascinating."

3. Reference in Ernst Käsemann, *New Testament Questions of Today*, trans. W. J. Montague (Philadelphia: Fortress Press, 1969), 109, introductory note. The context was Käsemann's debate with his critics over the issue of "primitive" Christian apocalyptic and his insistence on going back to the original texts in the New Testament.

4. Some more recent discussion on this point can be found, with references, in the volume jointly edited by Charlesworth and myself, *Images of Jesus Today*, Faith and Scholarship Colloquies (Valley Forge, Pa.: Trinity Press International, 1994); esp. see my Foreword, xvii.

5. See n. 1. See especially the discussion on pp. 131–36. The work gives a fine account of the newer discoveries and their bearing on the whole question of the historical Jesus.

6. An early, summarizing article is that by Marcus Borg, "A Renaissance in Jesus Studies," *Theology Today* 45 (1988): 280–92. See also the splendid condensation of current research by James H. Charlesworth in *Images of Jesus Today*, chap. 1, as well as the chapter by Borg in the same volume (chap. 2).

7. Above, n. 1.

8. Sanders, *Jesus and Judaism*.

9. Burton Mack, *A Myth of Innocence* (Philadelphia: Fortress Press, 1988). See also his more recent *The Lost Gospel: The Book of Q and Christian Origins* (San Francisco: Harper, 1993) for a relating of the Q Community to the Cynic movement.

10. John Dominic Crossan, *The Historical Jesus: The Life of a Mediterranean Jewish Peasant* (San Francisco: Harper, 1991).

11. The case is set out with great clarity by Marcus Borg in *Images of Jesus Today* (chap. 2).

12. There are obvious exceptions in the Vatican censures of the work by Hans Küng, Edward Schillebeeckx, or, in this country, Charles Curran. They only show how odd such affairs appear in the modern-day academy.

13. The Jesus Seminar seems to have a high place on its agenda for disseminating the results of critical inquiry into the historical

Jesus question and gains access to the popular media with some regularity. The publication of its evaluation of the *logoi* tradition was accompanied by some public fanfare. The work is *The Five Gospels: The Search for the Authentic Words of Jesus,* New Translation and Commentary by Robert W. Funk, Roy W. Hoover, and the Jesus Seminar (A Polebridge Press Book; New York: Macmillan Publishing Company, 1993).

14. How historical "fact" and theological "truths" might be related now involves being somewhat informed about archaeological discoveries; and in this connection see the volumes jointly edited by Charlesworth and myself, *What Has Archaeology to Do with Faith?* Faith and Scholarship Colloquies (Philadelphia: Trinity Press International, 1992).

Index of Authors and Subjects